ROBIN LOWES

# THE
# INCOMPLEAT
# ANGLER

*A light cast over river and loch*

ROBIN LOWES

# THE INCOMPLEAT ANGLER

## A light cast over river and loch

THIRD MILLENNIUM PUBLISHING

© 1999 Robin Lowes

British Library Cataloguing in Publication Data:
A catalogue record for this book is available
from the British Library

ISBN 0 9536969 0 1

Published in the UK in 1999 by
Third Millennium Publishing Limited
Shawlands Court
Newchapel Road
Lingfield
Surrey RH7 6BL

1 3 5 7 9 8 6 4 2

Set in Photina
Designed and produced by Pardoe Blacker Limited
Lingfield · Surrey

Colour origination by Colour Books, Hong Kong
Printed in Slovenia

# Contents

# Acknowledgements

I AM IMMENSELY GRATEFUL to Lord Nickson for his extremely generous Foreword. He has been in the forefront of the battle to save the Atlantic salmon ever since it became threatened. A member of the Council of the Atlantic Salmon Trust since 1982, he was its Chairman for eight years and is currently Vice-President. He has also been Chairman of the North Atlantic Salmon Fund (UK) from 1993 to 1997, and the Chairman of the Secretary of State for Scotland's Salmon Strategy Task Force from 1995 to 1997. In addition, he has served on the Council of the Association of Scottish Fishery Boards since 1980 and has been its President since 1996.

A member of the Salmon and Trout Association for 30 years, he has been a lifelong fisherman, and as he so delightfully puts it, just loves salmon. This love, on both sides of his family, goes a very long way back and his earliest copy of *The Compleat Angler* bears his great-great grandfather's signature in 1828. The Fishmongers Company, in recently making him an Honorary Freeman 'in recognition of outstanding services to the conservation and management of the wild salmon over many years' says it all. We owe him – salmon included – an immense debt of thanks for his dedication to their survival.

I must also thank Mitch Campbell, the executive assistant to the President of the Moisie Salmon Club and James Houghton, the current President, for their help and for keeping me up to date on the Moisie River; to Lord Tryon, Aylmer Tryon's nephew for allowing me to quote from Aylmer's *The Quiet Waters By* and for furnishing me with details of catches on the River Frome that go back well before the war; to Paul Torday for his help and comments on the North Tyne; to Don and Ann Calder for inviting us to fish the Miramichi in New Brunswick, and to my eldest son Anthony for his splendid chapters on the Bighorn River, Montana, and his recent experiences fishing the Rynda near Murmansk on the Kola Peninsula. To Rodger McPhail for allowing me to use his extremely witty cartoon at the end of the Chalk Streams chapter, and finally, I must thank Elwyn Blacker for his tremendous enthusiasm and help along with that of his staff without which this book would never have reached the net.

# DEDICATION

*This book is dedicated to my wife Bobby*
*whose support, encouragement and enthusiasm*
*as a camp follower – and dare I say it, cook –*
*has driven her to verse:*

TALES OF A FISHERMAN'S WIFE

*My wife, poor wretch as Pepys would say,*
*As she sits on the bank day by day,*
*And after hours she has to listen*
*To the size of the fish that got away –*
*Larger and larger they seem to get*
*But there is no proof without a net.*

*She should be called the Lady in Waiting*
*As she sits and waits with breath abaiting.*
*I could have caught that fish she may think*
*As she sits there immobile without any drink.*
*A whisky or so would not come amiss!*
*She may then think the day has been bliss.*
*What a lovely happy partnership to book,*
*One is the boss and the other the cook.*

# Foreword

*By* THE LORD NICKSON KBE DL

ROBIN LOWES is a brilliant amateur photographer. He cares deeply about wildlife and is a born naturalist with an abiding love of the countryside.

Anyone who remembers his photographs on the cover of *The Field* or has a copy of his previous books *Tales of Four Seasons* and *Field Sports and the Countryside* will know that they are in for a veritable feast.

*The Incompleat Angler* is a splendid title for a splendid book. But those who know Robin will agree that with his usual modesty he has underplayed both his great expertise as a fisherman and his wide fishing experience. He takes us on a series of exciting fishing expeditions with his fine descriptive writing and magical photographs from his home territory in the highlands of Scotland to the softer landscapes of the south country chalk streams. We visit with him and his friends the North Tyne and the Helmsdale before embarking on a mouth-watering pilgrimage to some of the most exclusive Atlantic salmon rivers in the world – the Hofsa in Iceland and the Moisie and the Miramichi in Canada.

His son Anthony has added chapters on two very different rivers – the Bighorn in Montana, and the Rynda in the Kola Peninsula in Russia. In both places he describes fishing first for trout and then for salmon of a quality and abundance of which most of us can only dream.

We can enjoy in words and pictures Robin Lowes acute observation of birds and animals, varying from eagles to deer, ptarmigan to phalaropes, bustards to beavers and water voles to wagtails.

There are many sorts of fishing books and most fishermen are addicted to them all. But there is a special indulgence in taking a book like this, that unashamedly seeks to entertain by reminiscence rather than to instruct, to the winter fireside to revel in the fabulous fishing experiences of others.

And this book is indeed a delight. The text alone would find a worthy place on most fishing bookshelves, but coupled with the outstanding illustrations the author and publishers have given us a rare treat.

This is a book which will be read and re-read, recommended to friends but rarely lent for fear of losing it!

The search for this year's Christmas present is over.

DAVID NICKSON

# Introduction

IT WAS IN A HAPPY HUNTING GROUND OF LOCHS AND RIVERS in the south-west corner of Perthshire and adjoining Argyll that I had the good fortune to be brought up to the arts of trout fishing from the very early age of six.

Fishing the River Fillan just below the White Bridge the following year when I was seven – or rather attempting to do so, for I had no idea how to set about it, having never used anything but a pole with a bit of string and a bent pin baited with bread with which my brother and I had hauled out many luckless roach in a Surrey pond – I was approached by a man who asked how I was getting on. Knowing the answer even before I could reply, he produced from his creel what I thought at the time a monster trout – it must have weighed all of twelve ounces – and told me in that delightfully soft West Highland accent I was to get to know so well, to take it back and tell my father I had caught it! My father naturally enough guessed the truth sooner than it was uttered but it was to such actions that small boys respond and I became a fishing fanatic from that day on.

When I was fifteen a nearby estate came on the market and in November 1933 my father bought it. Our sporting horizons immediately extended beyond our wildest dreams to include a small sea trout river, deer, grouse, golden eagles, ptarmigan on the tops and a wealth of other wildlife. Two years later I caught my first salmon – on a very small Silver Doctor, – but I had to wait many years before catching another one!

I realize how wonderfully lucky I have been to fish so many of the most intriguing and famous rivers of the world and it is about these later exploits that the subsequent chapters have been written. The fly fishers' motto really hits the nail on the head in no uncertain terms for there is surely 'so much more to fishing than catching fish'.

# Highland homespun –
# a spate river

OURS IS A SPATE RIVER in the strictest sense of the word – it has no loch at its source to augment its natural flow. But given six hours continuous heavy rain it is transformed from a mere trickle to a roaring torrent that would have been unimaginable a few hours earlier as water pours down from the steep hills on either side, some of which are over 3,000 ft high. When the rain stops it clears extraordinarily quickly, and many times fishermen have been caught out, not realising just how quickly the main chance comes and goes. It is a short river – barely a mile and a half of fishable water as the Upper Falls brings all running fish to a full stop by its unjumpable height – but above this barrier another four miles of water is fed by countless rivulets and burns, many of which dry up completely in fine weather.

From the end of May, given sufficient water, sea trout run up from the loch below and on very rare occasions the odd salmon, but it is in no sense a salmon river, nor did nature ever intend it to be. If we are lucky we might catch one perhaps every seven or eight years! Rock pools, rapids and waterfalls form the upper reaches, whilst below the Lower Falls, a series of less spectacular, though no less picturesque, longer broader pools flow through fields with woods on either side.

It was whilst fishing the Bridge Pool that runs parallel – and uncomfortably close to – the main road, at the height of a full spate many years ago, that my father unwittingly caused a monumental traffic jam by hooking and playing a splendid fish. As one car after another pulled up to watch the fun only the fortuitous arrival of an AA Scout, resplendent on yellow and black motor bike and side car, saved utter chaos as he nobly stepped into the breach to bring some semblance of order back to an extremely narrow main road. My father's American 8-ft Leonard rod – which so many Englishmen then coveted just as Americans coveted the Hardy equivalent – proved altogether too light for a river in full spate with a heavy fish on the other end. He was soon surrounded by car loads of well-wishers, some of

OPPOSITE:
*The Oak Tree Pool in full spate.*

13

whom volunteered quite helpful comments – 'why don't 'e pull it in' and 'I can't see t' float' being but two!

The fish, not to be outdone, made several nerve tingling runs, culminating in splendid three foot leaps, luckily stopping just short of the bridge on each occasion. Using the heavy water as big fish know how it was not finally netted until forty-five minutes of stress and struggle had elapsed. It proved to be a very large brown trout of 5¾lb. Its replica now hangs in the Lodge hall below the model of a 23lb salmon he caught even earlier, in the Kinglas Falls – a large salmon for such a gem of a small highland river that joins the Orchy at the Junction Pool; fishing then available through the Royal Hotel, Tyndrum.

Many years later these two fish were joined by another large brown trout of 5¼lb caught in the Bridge Pool, this time below the bridge, on a size 10 Jock Scott. On this occasion I had only one onlooker who witnessed the fun from the bridge, and asked while I was playing it, in a rather guttural accent if he could help net it for me. 'Have you ever netted a fish before?' I asked him and when he replied in the negative I almost said no thank you! But he seemed keen to have a go, and promised to do exactly as I told him and he netted it perfectly. It transpired that he was a student from Berlin University. I could not help reflecting that a few years earlier we could have been taking pot shots at each other, for the war was only just over. He was, however, as delighted with my success as I was – such is life!

The view from the Lodge at any time is always beautiful – after heavy and prolonged rain it is spectacular. It also gives us a splendid indication of the state of the river, for the Falls opposite are a marvellous guide as to whether it is worth going out before breakfast to try one's luck, and gives a good indication of the height of the river throughout the day. After a week without rain the Falls almost disappear.

Sea trout run up from late May onwards, the best runs being July, August and September, when, up to the time UDN struck in 1972 the Lower Falls would be moving with jumping fish trying desperately to reach the upper pools and side burns to spawn whenever a good spate occurred. I can sit and watch them for hours. Runs held up well for many years, but when the salmon disease arrived from Ireland our sea trout were very

*The view from the Lodge at any time is always beautiful – after heavy and prolonged rain it is spectacular.*

badly affected and considerable mortality was caused. As all fishermen know it was a wretched sight and for the first year or two the disease decimated sea trout as well as salmon. I was up with Jeremy, my second son, in mid-October, the year it struck us and the weather was perfect. Our Bridge Pool, both above and below the bridge, was stuffed with fish and it was rather like watching fish in an aquarium. The majority then seemed healthy but one very large sea trout had a very bad 'go' of the disease and was obviously dying. Jeremy managed to harpoon it and not only put it out of its misery but hopefully prevented it from infecting others. It weighed 11¼lb – a most depressing sight. The experts, who had been involved from the start in Ireland, said sea trout were badly affected for the first year but seemed to get over it more quickly than salmon. It killed a lot of fish and the runs have never really recovered to their former numbers though strangely we were, until recently, getting larger fish. Because of the effects of the disease we started a small hatchery, catching up our own stock where possible. We had often seen very large sea trout jumping the Lower Falls and guessed their weight at around 14–15lb, but had never caught anything heavier than 11½lb, a heavy sea trout in anyone's book. One year we had a problem catching up cock fish to fertilise the hen fish waiting in a holding pool, when Davie, our gamekeeper, who was getting desperate,

*Davie stripping a female sea trout of ova.*

*'I can sit and watch them for hours.' A very large sea trout jumping the Lower Falls.*

netted a cock fish of 16 lb in the Bridge Pool. Just to prove the point he caught two others of 14 and 15 lb the following season. These fish had obviously known the closing date for the season because they all ran up in November!

As all fishermen know sea trout numbers, especially along the west and north-west coast of Scotland – wherever fish farming is taking place – have plummeted in recent years, due to the proliferation of sea lice which attack salmon and sea trout smolts as they go out to sea. The attacks on young fish are so severe they either succumb or return to fresh water and it has had a devastating effect on them. Our river has suffered too but not for this reason for we have no fish farming, thank goodness, in our estuary. The last year ('98) has been a disastrous one, despite having wonderful water

*A 'breakfast' fish. Moira's 11¾lb salmon caught in the Corner Pool.*

conditions, so after an enforced gap of several years we have started up our hatchery again; it fell into disuse when Davie left. Perhaps his previous effort to supplement numbers was more effective than we realised.

I have always loved fishing before breakfast, given the right conditions, and several 'breakfast' fish have made the start of the day a truly memorable one. Moira and John, two guests, had arrived on a Sunday one September and as luck would have it we awoke on Monday to a river in full spate – time to be up and after them. I took Moira down to the Lower Pools, which at 8 a.m. were just perfect, whilst John went higher up. The river was high but settling and as she fished down the Corner Pool, a misnomer if ever there was one for it is straight as a die, a large fish jumped twenty or thirty yards below us. Two more casts I said and you'll cover it, and with the words barely uttered, a mighty swirl engulfed her fly and gave her a very exciting 15 minutes, made the more so by the heavy water, until I managed, at the second attempt, to net what proved to be a beautifully shaped salmon of 11³/₄lb – the first salmon any of us had caught out of the river for 18 years. It turned out to be ladies day with a vengeance for another of our lady guests caught a 9¹/₂lb sea trout, fishing with Davie in the Farm Pool, a pool he always thinks is the best on the river.

But it is the infinite variety from the Upper Falls down that lends such fascination to such a short river. It is home to much wildlife, some of it welcome, like our otters, but mink are definitely not. They put in an appearance many years ago – in the late 60s. I saw my first when I was fishing one of our top pools. It was ambling slowly along the opposite bank, and I must confess, with the sun shining on its glossy, almost jet black fur, it made a beautiful picture, but they are lethal predators of nearly all river life, birds and small mammals included. We saw it again two days later and immediately set about trying to trap it, without immediate success. Like otters they are great travellers, here today, gone tomorrow. We were on the point of going south ourselves ten days later when Davie arrived and laid a large black mink on the front doorstep. It looked identical to the one we had seen. 'Where did you get it?' I asked? He couldn't prevent a half smile from creasing his face as he replied 'in Alex's hen house'. It had killed eight hens and was found curled up asleep in the morning amongst its victims.

Our fun-loving otter is an altogether different animal. Never exactly numerous and seldom seen except perhaps at dusk or dawn, they have been with us ever since I can remember. My father was fortunate enough

*The Upper Falls in January 1941 – one of the coldest spells for years.*

in the severe winter of '41 to witness a family of otters tobogganing down a steep snow-covered bank and revelling in their particular form of winter sports – watching them play for almost half an hour. On another occasion my son Jeremy, fishing one side of our Lower Falls pool, was joined by an otter on the rocks the other side, before it too went fishing and disappeared into the foam beneath the Falls. He never saw whether it was more successful than he was. In the last few months an otter, to our delight, has made his holt amongst the roots of a huge oak tree by the side of one of the Lower Pools. One June evening a line of bubbles indicated his presence as he fished the length of the Bridge Pool, then climbed out on to a large rock just a few feet below the bridge itself where he proceeded to make his supper off a small trout he had just caught. When the river is frozen over their movements are always easier to see. One January a dusting of snow had powdered the same ice-covered pool to reveal the tracks of two otters as clearly as engraving on frosted glass, where they had walked together the entire length of the pool and separated briefly before joining up again as they made their way upstream.

The river at this time of year is at its most beautiful after a prolonged cold spell with hard night frosts and temperatures seldom above freezing

My 9 lb 2 oz sea trout from the Fank Pool. A scale sample of this fish was sent to Andrew Walker of the Freshwater Fisheries Laboratory, Faskally, Pitlochry. Their analysis indicated it was a sea trout, aged approximately 3.0+ 7sm+ (10+), i.e., it had migrated to sea as a three-year-old smolt and then spawned in the same year as a finnock, whitling or herling, then on a further six annual occasions.

during the day. Then steep-sided banks, oozing moisture, and the edges of waterfalls become festooned with icicles often many feet long, and where the water flows more slowly it freezes across whole pools, often forming a partial bridge on which to cross to the opposite bank. Sunlight after a heavy snowfall transforms the scene to one of sparkling beauty and the clarity of the air has a strange effect on distances, making them seem much closer than they really are, as with stars on a cloudless frosty night.

As winter gives way to the longer daylight hours of spring, the glen fills up with a remarkable wealth of migrants – grey wagtails and sandpipers up and down the river, redstarts, pied and spotted flycatchers, tree pipits, sand martins nesting in the shingle pool bank and many others. Kingfishers are an infrequent spring and summer visitor, and after a gap of a few years are back. It is a marvellous sight to see that vivid flash of blue and red wing-

*Fishing the Oak Tree Pool in perfect conditions.*

*An 8lb sea trout caught on a shrimp fly.*

ing its way up or downstream when fishing. Indeed fishing would be less than half the fun without all the animal and bird life that share the riverside.

After over 75 years it is interesting to look back even further to a comparison of catches made in the year 1866 and a hundred years later which revealed almost identical numbers of sea trout caught and the largest fish then recorded of around 7 1/2 lb. Larger fish were being caught until recently, when both size and numbers have fallen drastically. Let us hope it is only temporary.

I cannot end my short chapter without mentioning the Fank Pool, always considered for many years our best. It has provided marvellous sport and when we want a guest to catch a fish, he or she has been despatched there.

Last September, having not fished there myself all day, I thought I might give it a quick cast or two before dark. The river was in full spate and it was a horrible evening, rain teeming down, cold and almost dark when I arrived. I started at the neck of the pool and then noticed two girls half way down on the opposite bank, one in the river at the water's edge, the other about to join her – both completely naked, washing themselves with a bar of soap! They weren't exactly spoiling the pool but must have been getting an extraordinarily cold dip with shower above – the best of both worlds! As I fished my way down towards them I thought one more cast and I'll hook one – she'd have looked good in the Lodge Hall!

# Salad days on the Loch

OPPOSITE:
*Autumn glory! Many years ago ospreys probably nested on this, the Loch's most northen island.*

BELOW:
*Wild goats resting on the bank of Loch Lomond. You don't always see them – but you can certainly smell them!*

AFTER TWO WEEKS without rain the river was gin clear and down to a trickle; on these occasions we are fortunate to turn to one of Scotland's most famous lochs, if not exactly in the fishing sense, certainly in a scenic one. Many will guess I refer to Loch Lomond and its bonnie bonnie banks. Its northern end is spectacular, with ground rising almost vertically for 800–1000 feet for several miles along its north-eastern shore. Densely wooded low down with oak, birch and rowan, home to much wildlife from red and roe deer to wild goats that belie their name for they are remarkably tame and approachable; you may not always see them, but you are certain to smell them, given an unfavourable wind!

With the occasional sight of golden eagle, peregrine and buzzard thrown in, the observant fisherman has plenty to occupy his mind as his outboard

propels him close inshore around the bays where he may drift and fly fish or troll up and down the loch. Fishing the tap end as the locals call it, can be a most frustrating and monotonous game were it not for the beauty of the surroundings for it must be said that salmon and sea trout are few and far between, and this end cannot compare with the broader lower half of the loch with its many islands and famous Endrick bank and river. The present sad decline often serves to recall incidents of past glory or disaster as we pass over the very spot where these events occurred, in the hope that history might repeat itself.

Years ago I had somewhat rashly, and with tongue in cheek, asked over tea who would like to accompany me that evening on to the loch to catch a salmon – a quick troll round the bays was all we had time for. I must add that although trying on many occasions we had never yet succeeded in catching one, a fact of which most of my friends were only too well aware. I remember this suggestion was greeted with marked lack of enthusiasm by most of the party, but having had a very sporting and successful short day after snipe and duck, two good friends, Pat and Henry, volunteered to accompany me. Some year or two earlier I had been given an unusual looking minnow – a natural minnow encased in clear plastic, one side natural colour, the other coloured vermilion. I had been assured it was a most deadly lure, proven successful by two ardent fishermen on Loch Lubnaig, but I had never tried it until that evening. This I mounted on my very old Greenheart sea trout rod, the other rod having a more orthodox golden sprat.

We had covered virtually all our usual water and ·were heading for home, when Pat asked what I thought the odds were on catching a salmon now. Fifty to one I said, and with the words scarcely uttered it happened – a magnificent salmon bent my Greenheart almost in half, porpoised out of the water and streaked off on a run of at least eighty yards. Pat, who was holding the rod, let out a screech as the reel fell off its ill-fitting ring attachment and danced a fantastic jig as more and more line was torn off. How it didn't end then and there I shall never know, but seizing the rod and catching the reel I managed somehow to get it back into its fitting and regained control. I handed the rod back to Pat and our salmon proceeded to repeat the performance with another electrifying run of a good fifty yards; then exactly the same thing happened. This was too much for Pat whose excitement had reached fever pitch. Handing the rod back to me she refused to have anything more to do with it! But fortune was with us and our salmon,

OPPOSITE:
*Trolling round the tap end of Loch Lomond – no ripple, no fish!*

26

growing more dignified, decided to try for the bottom rather than the opposite shore – and the bottom thereabouts is no mean depth. My sea trout rod was now bent double and I remember wondering just how long it would stand the strain. For the next twenty minutes, however, it remained agonisingly intact and with infinite care I coaxed our salmon towards the boat. In our haste to be out after tea we had forgotten a gaff – they were legal in those days, but we never thought we would need one anyway – but fortunately had a fair sized net which I was sure would serve equally well. We battled on, worrying more about whether the rod would snap than anything else, and as the minutes ticked by the inches rewound themselves on to the reel, until at last our salmon lay within reach.

There is nothing like netting a fish at the first attempt, especially as on many occasions the first chance is often the last. Our horror can be imagined when the salmon failed completely to go into the net. One touch of the net and new life surged through it and for another ten minutes our monster – for it was fast becoming that – lay immovable on the loch bottom.

Tension cannot last indefinitely without something giving way and once again our salmon was inched towards the net and once again it failed to go in. The drama that followed really should have been filmed.

Henry, casting net aside, leant far out over the side of the boat and with legs held firmly by his wife Pat, reached out and getting both hands under it lifted it into the boat like a baby. It weighed exactly 15 lb – some baby! After this success we had to wait quite a time for our next salmon, and this still remains to date the heaviest we have caught and, without doubt, the most exciting.

It has always been our aim to catch one in the loch on a fly and whenever it is feasible, and conditions allow, I or one of my friends fly fish from the bows when trolling. We also fly fish certain likely looking drifts along beautifully shelving gravelly banks, where of course there is always the chance of rising a sea trout as well.

It was in doing just this with a boat load of children and fishing a size 10 single-hook Thunder and Lightning, one of my favourite flies, that with a strong north wind blowing us far too quickly over one perfect shelving bank, a sea trout rose to my Thunder with the most monumental swirl. I was then on the receiving end of a quite magnificent tussle which took out, on its first run – and before we could stop and get the boat under any sort of control – almost every yard of my line and backing. But having survived

*Pat's 15 pounder.*

*The triumphant fisherwoman with her 8¹/₂lb sea trout.*

the first hurdle and ten more minutes of excitement in which the children joined – to control them in the boat was no small feat – our sea trout came up to the surface and planed along the trough of the waves for a good ten yards, before diving deep. For a second time it came up broadside to us and we could see every detail, its size and particularly beautiful markings. With net ready I thought one more dive and we'll have you, but with that thought scarcely formed it dived again – to freedom! With a sickening flick the rod straightened as the fly lost its hold on what was without question the largest Loch Lomond sea trout I have every hooked. I have never minded losing a fish, but I would dearly love to have known his weight – not less than 8 lb, maybe even 10, who knows? It gets heavier every year!

When we first fished Loch Lomond – and I can only refer to the northern end – we were given great help and encouragement by one of the locals who had his own boat and used to fish whenever he could, throughout the spring and summer evenings. He always maintained that salmon kept closest to the shore and that sea trout could be found further out. I remember he said you will sometimes see boats fishing in the middle of the loch – quite pointless, as they'll never catch a salmon there. One day we decided to cross the loch and fish down the other bank so, remembering his words, we turned the throttle up on our Seagull Outboard to get across as quickly as possible. When we were exactly half way over we hooked and landed a salmon of 6¾ lb. Isn't there always an exception to prove the rule!

OPPOSITE: *Loch Lomond, with Ben Lomond in the background, in early spring after a snowfall.*

BELOW: *A family of goosanders, lethal predators of salmon fry and other small fish – not a welcome sight to fishermen.*

# West Highlands – Rivers Orchy and Awe

CERTAIN EVENTS stamp themselves clearly in one's mind, especially when very young. Whilst staying at the Royal Hotel Tyndrum in Perthshire in September, when I was nine, we returned from the hill to find the most colossal salmon lying on the marble floor of the hall; this was a delightful custom whenever anything of note was caught. It was a truly magnificent fish, caught in the River Orchy by Duncan Fraser who lived in a cottage half way down the glen. He had caught it on a fly – a Silver Wilkinson – behind a rock in what I believe was called the Shepherd's Pool, and weighed 44 lb. Almost exactly a year later, in the same pool, behind the same rock, on the same fly he caught another, this time of 41 lb.

Such were the monsters of those far-off days now all but vanished. Of course the Orchy had, and still has, the potential for big fish, running as it does into Loch Awe and then by the River Awe through the Pass of Brander down countless rapids, some lost forever to the hydroelectric dam, to the sea. For the Awe itself has a wonderful big fish record, but how often these days is a fish of over 40 lb caught, let alone two in successive seasons in the same pool?

We were not to see the second of those magnificent salmon for a year later we had to vacate the hotel in a hurry along with everyone else when it caught fire during the evening. A candle too close to a net curtain in the staff quarters started it all, and the fire took an instant hold, fanned by strong winds. When the nearest fire engine arrived from over 50 miles distance their hoses wouldn't reach the almost dried up burn to the hotel and that was that. The hotel was completely gutted. My brother had somehow managed to 'guddle' a 3/4 lb brown trout out of a nearby burn, which he had been promised would be cooked specially for his breakfast – and so it was – to a cinder, ten hours ahead of time!

It was many years later that I had the considerable pleasure of fishing the Orchy and Kinglas, which joined the Orchy at the Junction Pool, and watching salmon and grilse jumping the Kinglas Falls. This was the pool where my father caught his large salmon on a Jock Scott, and was saved

OPPOSITE:
*Wading one of the lower pools of the River Awe.*

*The Kinglas Falls Pool
viewed from above.*

from being eaten alive by midges whilst playing it for almost an hour by his pipe smoke – no insect repellents were remotely effective in those days.

When in the 'fifties' I had the chance of fishing the Orchy and Kinglas myself it did not take us long to jump at the chance offered to us by the then owner of Auch, whose sheep farm nestles at the foot of Ben Dorian. I felt it was almost home from home for we are only a short distance away, and Glen Orchy is without doubt one of the most beautiful Glens in the Western Highlands. All the locals never dreamt of using anything but a worm – or spinning – and when one of them joined us and saw me fly fishing he thought I was mad, and very nearly said so. Fortunately I was able to show him I wasn't, pointing to a small salmon I had just caught on a Thunder and Lightning, lying on the bank. I remember he really thought I was pulling his leg, and only believed me when Brian Duncan, our keeper confirmed it! Many pools provide lovely fly water – he didn't know what he was missing.

With Loch Tulla at its head the Orchy stays very fishable for several days after heavy rain, with help from the Kinglas which joins it at the Junction Pool just below Bridge of Orchy. We considered the Junction Pool probably the best on our beat though it would be hard to choose between the Otter, Farm, Rock and Colonel's Pool – by August nearly all held fish. Sitting on the bank looking down on both Junction and Farm Pools in August it was not long before one would see a salmon 'flash' its side or splash out of the water, but they could prove very dour. I cannot recall who suggested I should get my labrador to swim through the Junction Pool to wake them up and then throw a fly over it after a ten minute breather. But I did try throwing a prawn across and then caught a beauty of a ten pounder on a small Thunder and Lightning almost immediately afterwards – though it only worked once!

One April – for many years the best month for the lower pools on the Orchy before spring runs collapsed so disastrously everywhere, and made worse by the hydro-electric scheme on the Awe – we were offered a day's

*The Otter Pool on the Orchy – beautiful fly water.*

fishing near Dalmally. This is the only time I have ever fished the lower Orchy pools. There was plenty of water from the snow melt and with Brian Duncan who had previously had five years of experience on the Navar in Sutherland we had almost given up hope when I hooked a salmon well down in the middle of the Succoth Pool with a size 2/0 Gary. Anthony, my eldest son, had tied this, aged 14$\frac{1}{2}$, as well as any professional fly-tyer. I remember that his brother Jeremy had discovered a mass of little elvers wriggling their way upstream close to the shore. At this time of year there may still be a few kelt about that have not yet returned to the sea, and neither Brian nor I were sure I hadn't hooked one. It fought long and well, and when we eventually landed it, it proved in beautiful condition but not the colour of a fresh springer. On close examination we discovered it was a baggot, a salmon that had failed to spawn after running up the previous

*The beauty of the River Awe near Taynuilt.*

*In his seventh heaven!*

*The Awe – one of the lower pools as it runs down towards Loch Etive.*

autumn. On even closer inspection we found what seemed to be the cause – a gaff mark, completely healed, near its ventral fin. Whether it had escaped capture or how it happened will always remain a mystery. Its flesh was a rich pink and it ate superbly.

Poaching for a period on the upper beat was a bit of a problem despite lots of 'notices'. Years later, fishing the top pools with a great friend, he found his pool occupied by two lads of about 10–12 years old who had no right to be there. Having suitably admonished them, he proceeded to give them a lesson in fly casting for, as he put it later, he didn't want to put them off fishing for the rest of their lives! It was typical of him. Little did they know they were receiving a lesson from one of the finest fishermen in the land, Aylmer Tryon.

In recent years much of the Glen has been spoilt by fir plantations that have now grown up to screen the river. On a recent drive up the Glen it was impossible to recognise or even see the pools we used to fish. Worse still these plantations are bound to have a detrimental effect on the acidity of the water, and thus the fishing – just as the hydroelectric scheme and barrage on the Awe has affected what was left of the spring run. Sadly, the Awe is now just a shadow of its former self, typical of so many other salmon rivers. What a wretched way to end a description of what was for so many years one of the most famous West Highland salmon rivers.

# The Frome

THE RIVER FROME SNAKES ITS WAY through the lush water meadows of Dorset to enter the sea at Poole Harbour. It is a small fast flowing river, quite deep in places, as it twists and turns and doubles back on itself as if it is almost reluctant to leave the land it has just passed.

It was to this totally new scene that I was introduced by Aylmer Tryon in the early fifties when we first met and became firm friends, from then on fishing together in Scotland, and many other parts of the world including the Sustut in North British Columbia. I think I must have fished the Frome as his guest every year from our first meeting. We stayed first at Woolbridge Manor on the banks of the Frome, and then Kingfisher Mill, about which he has written so delightfully – and of the Frome too – in *The Quiet Waters By*.

It was whilst staying at Woolbridge Manor and fishing after supper one summer evening many years ago that I had an intriguing experience of seeing how a salmon sometimes takes a prawn, a lure we were allowed to use in those days before they were banned because they proved so deadly.

Fishing, just below the railway bridge on the narrow path against a ledge on the west bank, now completely overgrown, I cast out my prawn. I was just watching it spin slowly against the current about ten feet below me when a large salmon came up from the depths and took it gently in its mouth. I struck at the precise moment that the salmon opened its mouth and the prawn came whistling out into the air making no contact whatsoever. I cast again and exactly the same thing happened. I paused to think for a second, then cast again, bringing the prawn up through the water at treble the speed and my salmon took with a wallop! After fifteen minutes or so of alarms and excursions it proved a beauty of 24½lb.

Once Kingfisher Mill had been built – a quite unique mill house on the Wiltshire Avon, we surely had the best of both worlds. If it had been raining all night and the Frome proved too dirty, we simply turned to his beautiful stretch of trout water, went up to feed the bustards he was so keen to re-introduce to Salisbury Plain, mowed his lawn or helped weed his garden. Or we simply watched the wealth of wildlife through the huge picture window of his living room that looked down on a portion of the Avon that had been deflected through the mill race under his house. Then we would take

*The result of a sea lamprey on a salmon caught above the Bunny; it did nothing to deter its fighting prowess.*

*The bustards which Aylmer Tryon was so determined to re-introduce to Salisbury Plain.*

up our trout rods for the evening rise. There was in truth never a dull moment! But the Frome – and salmon fishing – was an altogether new experience from the trout and sea trout fishing I had been brought up to in the Scottish Highlands – and equally fascinating. If we were there in early spring we could always count on seeing our first swallow. Sandmartins arrived there mid-March and by the third week of May if we were lucky we would see a hobby, that beautiful little migrant falcon, sometimes quite close, as it flew over the river catching mayflies and clearing the area temporarily – and very quickly – of martins and swallows.

Fishing's first port of call was invariably the Bunny, a low double-arched ten-foot cattlebridge where salmon rested after running up through the weir hatches of the Mill Pool. Hooking a salmon just above the Bunny, it was short odds on the fish deciding to beat it through the bridge and back in to the Mill Pool. When this happened the problem – or one of them! – was to keep the fish and rod on the same side of the Bunny.

Anthony Tryon, Aylmer's nephew, has very kindly given me permission to use the following accounts from *The Quiet Waters By*, for which I am most grateful, for they really are too good to miss:

'The most successful fish was one which took a fly some fifty yards above the Bunny, near an ash tree, and then went down through one of the arches. My nephew Anthony ran down and jumped into the river above the hatches, to try to head it off. His labrador, not to be left out of the excitement, jumped in after him and was swept down. Anthony tried to grab him, lost his footing, but just managed to seize the beam over the hatches, so that only half of him went through where salmon and dog had disappeared. A few minutes later a very bedraggled retriever reappeared. As to the salmon, he was safely in the Mill Pool, having broken the cast, while the angler himself had broken his rod. This was indeed a piscatorial triumph for the fish!

Anthony, in early April 1963, hooked a large fish from the southern bank, which ran upstream. He followed as best he could, but we leave the trees and bushes on that bank to give cover for the fish, so he reached a point of no advance, the fish, by then, being up towards the railway bridge. After a long battle Anthony thought that he would be better on the *rive gauche*, and although the river was high and very cold, he waded up to his arm-pits and, luckily, reached the bank safely and landed his fish. He arrived at the hut for lunch, very cold, extremely wet, but triumphant, as the fish weighed 35 lb. We revived him with hot soup and whisky.

When a fish is hooked and goes through the Bunny Bridge, a partner is almost essential. There are three alternatives, one, to hook up the line below the bridge, and when there is no pull from the fish – usually because it has got off – cut the line and re-tie, then repeat the process in the Mill Pool, below the hatches; the second is, when all seems quiet, especially the reel, to hitch the line round the still silent reel, throw the rod into the river, having hooked the line below, and pull it out below the bridge, even if in pieces. Then again repeat at the hatches, which is even more hazardous for human, and for rod, especially if split cane. The third method was invented by Jonathan Heywood, *faute de mieux*, who in 1986, hooked three fish just above the Mill hatches, which, on each occasion, went straight down into the Mill Pool below. He let them run out much line – he really had little option – and then wedged his rod in a tree, fished up the line in the Mill Pool and played the fish by hand – surprisingly he won twice and lost once – a fish of over 20 lb, which broke him!'

*Swan – whose mate was known as Edgar – sitting on her eggs.*

One event that made a terrific stir was the arrival at the Bunny of a giant salmon one early May weekend. It lay just in the span of the northern arch and alongside it lay another salmon estimated at over 20 lb, which it completely dwarfed. This smaller salmon proved to weigh 22 lb because Anthony Tryon caught it! The giant refused all manner of flies and lures, but rose to one offering and was very clearly seen as it came right up to the surface – it was estimated to be in excess of 50 lb. Robert Hainard, the famous Swiss naturalist/artist was staying with Aylmer at the time and proceeded to sketch the scene of both salmon lying side by side, a water vole swimming right over them and the reflection of his own head and shoulders peering down. The moment has been preserved in one of his delightful woodcuts for which he was famous.

Before the war a salmon of 54lb had been caught on one of the beats below. A stone seat was erected by the pool in its honour with its huge outline engraved on it – there for all to see – what a pity this giant wasn't caught too. The Bunny could have done with a good seat.

For some years part of the river flowed down the salmon ladder into the salmon ladder pool which then looped round into the Mill Pool, thus by-passing the Bunny altogether. But there is no longer sufficient flow to divert or hold salmon there any more. One weekend before this Aylmer and I were inspecting the pool when we saw a very large fish show and Aylmer made me try for it with a fly. It wasn't interested. We forbore to try for it with a prawn, but on returning to the pool later that Saturday we tried for it again, first with a fly and then a yellowbelly and then returned to Kingfisher Mill. It was still there on Sunday but solemnly refused all offers again. I showed Aylmer a very small Silver Devon about half an inch long that had been lan-guishing in my tackle box for years. He didn't think much of it, and we left our prize in peace whilst we lunched at the hut and fished the lower pools until, on the way home, we decided to have one more go. In desperation Aylmer told me to try it with a prawn – still no reaction – so while he fished the Bunny a few yards across the field, I slipped on my tiny Silver Devon – and the salmon took it literally first cast!

While it roared round the salmon ladder pool twice very fast we could see quite clearly another fish that had stationed itself on its flank. I have had this happen in Scotland when I was playing a large sea trout. On the first circuit my line had picked up a streamer of weed hanging from the lip of the pool, which made straight line contact impossible. I think this had a bearing on what followed, for the salmon suddenly decided to leave the pool and I had to race after it – doing the long jump over a ditch which I just cleared in my effort to follow. I had nearly made it to the Mill Pool when my salmon tore off more line, did a splendid leap at the tail of the Mill Pool and threw my Devon out of its mouth in disgust! Not being able to maintain direct contact my line must have fouled the shallow centre of the pool as it

SEA TROUT   15½ pounds   .   15ᵀᴴ June 1981   KELT ALLEY   F
A.D. TRYON.

*Roger McPhail's painting of Aylmer Tryon's sea trout of 15½lb.*

*A view from the Hut Pool before spraying put paid to the buttercups.*

made off downstream. Aylmer thought it could easily have weighed 30 lb – I'd have settled for 25!

One of the things that pleased Aylmer a lot and pleased many of his friends even more – for he was an extraordinarily generous host, always sending you to the most likely pools on the river – was his catching of a 15½ lb sea trout on a shrimp fly. It was the most beautifully shaped fish, painted by Roger McPhail from an outline of the actual fish, and rather surprisingly for a sea trout was completely devoid of spots. This was a monster sea trout in anyone's book and I believe a second one of the same weight was caught the same week.

I must recall another weekend when Anthony, his nephew. who had recently returned from Australia joined us. Bobby, my wife, was doing her stuff cleaning out the hut – always welcome after the frequent comings and goings of numerous field mice had left their mark – when she saw Anthony playing a salmon in the Hut Pool. Aylmer and I were a long way upstream and saw nothing of the action, but after a time Anthony turned to Bobby and asked her to gaff his fish for him. 'No Anthony', she said 'I've never gaffed a fish before – but I'll play it for you and you can gaff it.' Without a word and with only the slightest flicker of an eye he handed her the rod – without doubt his finest hour, for I think he thought she had never played a fish before either! However, all went well and the photograph shows Anthony with his salmon – all 28¹/₂lb of it. He was not to know that she had in fact caught several large sea trout and a brown trout of 6³/₄lb in Scotland!

I must record two other incidents which occurred in reverse order. On arriving one morning after some rain during the night we found the river high and dirty but fishable. Having inspected it Aylmer said 'put on a large fly that they can see' and added as an afterthought 'and a strong cast in case you hook a big one.' I showed him a large light yellow winged fly – size 2, I think – with black and silver body, that I had been given years earlier and never used and whose name I have never known. I asked him what he thought of it, adding that at least they should see it. 'Yes', he said, 'that should do the trick' – and it did. Fishing from the opposite side of the river just below where many years earlier I had recounted the episode with the prawn, a salmon rose to my fly, pushing the water up rather as a submarine breaks the surface, and I knew, without seeing it, that I had hooked something pretty big. Aylmer, who was not far off, soon joined me and it was then that I was immensely grateful to his earlier comment to put on a strong cast, for after some minutes of working up stream it decided to go down. As it passed us both Aylmer's comment 'don't let it go down there you'll never get it' made me put on tremendous strain as I muttered 'easier said than done!' But to my immense relief and a 'well done' from Aylmer it turned and a few minutes later was safely on the bank. Neither of us quite realised how large it was, even when out of the water, but it weighed exactly 28¹/₂lb and I have never caught a larger.

The second incident occurred some years before. In years gone by when the Frome had splendid runs of salmon, the July summer runs usually produced fish of 8 to 10lb and I was not at all ready for the fish that took my prawn at the bottom of the Railway Pool some six to eight feet from the bank where I was standing. I was just on the point of drawing it out of the water when the giant of a salmon 'took' and lay on his side, right on the surface, beating the water with its huge tail – flop, flop, flop. Time just stood still whilst I looked at this huge fish – without doubt the largest I have ever hooked anywhere – for not only was it long, his depth was enormous. Heavens, what have I hooked I thought, and yelled to Aylmer who was fishing below and who did the 200 metres in record time to join me. The

*– all 28¹/₂lb of salmon.*

*Yet another 28¹/₂lb salmon caught on the River Frome; Aylmer holding up my giant.*

remainder of the story was a bit of an anticlimax, as my fish recovered its equilibrium and went deep down to the tail of the pool, and then went solid; we think it must have rounded a submerged fence post. There was no way of telling. It was all I could do to stop Aylmer from swimming across and taking my rod with him to see if he could clear the obstruction – maybe I should have done so myself. After an agonising ten minutes the prawn tackle came back with one hook completely straightened, and that was that – except, I must add, that maybe it is sometimes more fun to lose a huge fish than to catch it! After all you cannot boast about catching a monster for the rest of your life, whereas you can bore your friends to distraction with the story of the one that got away! You want to know how large it really was? So do I!

*The following records for the Bindon stretch of the Frome go back as far as 1926 when the Dwight family fished there for twenty years. The Tryon records take over in 1947 and I am immensely grateful to Lord Tryon, Aylmer's nephew, for giving me access to both. They make fascinating reading. Very little fishing was done by the Dwights after the month of May.*

*Massive spring salmon were nearly all caught in the months of March to April, and four in 1928 of over 30lb, two of them, 37lb each, were caught in March that year. In 1935 sixty-three salmon were caught, averaging 21lb a fish, and although the number fell to twenty-eight the following year (1936), the average weight rose to 22³/₄lb. Fishing stopped in those years at the end of June, voluntarily. After the war salmon numbers peaked at ninety-six for the season, averaging 13¹/₂lb in 1959, when fishing continued into September. Just under half of these were caught on a fly.*

*In the ten years of the fifties, five hundred and twenty-one salmon were caught at Bindon. This number fell to two hundred and sixty-six in the sixties and fell still further to one hundred and ninety. It will be remembered that drift netting started off Greenland in 1969.*

*In the 1980s only one hundred and thirty salmon were caught – an average of only 13 a year and in the last five years of the eighties this average actually fell to 2.9 a year – a disastrous decline. From 1990 to 1994 only ten salmon were caught, and none in the two years that followed. The English and Irish governments are the only two that have still not banned drift netting on the high seas. Res ipsa locquitur!*

# The North Tyne

ONE OF THE SUCCESS STORIES of recent years – there haven't been many – is the recovery of the River Tyne to being again one of the finest salmon rivers in England. Killed by industrial pollution for very many years, from the late 1930s its restoration to a pollution-free environment, despite a few hiccups, has shown what can be done by cleaning up a river – if not quite yet to its former glory, then certainly a step or two towards it.

It is always an exciting prospect to fish any river for the first time. In my case made doubly so, for my father was born and bred in Northumberland not far from Chipchase Castle near Wark where we were to fish, and near where he had spent the first twenty-five years of his life. It was completely unknown territory to me but we were soon to get to love it and realise what a remarkably beautiful county Northumberland is.

*A beautiful May day near Barrasford – a little on the low side for fishing.*

The river was, by mid-September, fairly well stocked with salmon and sea trout on our first ever visit. With just time for a quick fish before dark, my youngest son was fast into a salmon, in a likely looking stretch of fly water below the cottage where we were staying. He eventually landed a 12 lb salmon, a splendid way to start.

It is a beautiful river by anyone's standards, with magnificent beech trees lining the steep banks on the opposite side for much of our beat. I had almost completed fishing down the Straights – the topmost pool – one morning when I saw a tremendous splash – of a large fish I thought – some 300 yards below me. Mattie, the retired keeper who was looking after us, joined me as I was reeling in and asked me if I had seen the osprey! Yes, I said, realising immediately what I'd taken to be a salmon jumping; I wonder if it was more successful than me! Two ospreys in fact had made their home in the area that summer and we were to see them several times, on one occasion very close as one flew out of an oak tree just above my head. It had been everyone's hope that they would return the following year, but alas this has not happened – not yet at least.

There is one stretch of water almost opposite the cottage that looked particularly attractive. The river narrows from a wide stretch of shallow water and a small island accelerates the flow as it deepens and is drawn over to the opposite bank. It looked an absolute gem of a pool and perfect fly fishing water, except for the horrible hazard of a large broken branch of beech, which dangled down into the water a few yards from the opposite bank (it has now been removed). I had on my first visit had a splendid tussle with an 18½ pounder just above this spot. Now, early spring, a time of year when Mattie suggested it might well be worth trying – and apparently very few did – I had returned a year or two later for a weeks' fishing at the end of April with my wife and Aylmer Tryon. Aylmer by then was a bit unsteady on his pins, and had a problem wading, so Mattie was with him in case of need and, with Mattie, my large net. No gaffs allowed. They were fishing the Main Island Pool a few hundred yards below but out of sight of me. The river looked in pretty good order, and I had just reached the beech branch hanging down on the far bank when from the depths the most beautiful salmon grabbed my fly, a yellow shrimp fly, in an absolutely classic 'take'.

*Into a salmon at the Straights.*

Seeing the whole thing, always the most exciting moment, I was amazed I didn't lose it there and then by striking too soon and thus snatching the fly out of its mouth. But it felt solidly hooked as it ran back into deep water by the far bank and then upstream, passing perilously close to the branch hanging in the water. How it missed fouling my line I shall never know. Running upstream at a good pace I was forced to retrace my steps through the strong current; but eventually after many alarms and excursions, it had tired sufficiently for me to ponder where and how I was going to land it. The shingle above would have been ideal, but where I was it had become a bank of much larger rocks and stones. My additional problem was that I was wearing chest waders and a plastic cotton mackintosh, good for keeping the wet out, but not very good for bending. After two or three abortive and rather clumsy beaching attempts, I realised I would lose my prize if I went on like that so got down on hand and knees, and managed to get my free hand underneath it, scooping him out on to the bank like a bear. It

*A rare and beautiful goshawk – the deadly enemy of the red squirrel.*

*Looking upstream towards the Chipchase lower beat.*

weighed $22\frac{1}{2}$lb and proved the largest salmon caught at Chipchase that season. I suppose the moral to this story is – if you want to catch a big fish, lend someone your net!

We repeated our weeks' stay the following year in early May, without I may add catching another $22\frac{1}{2}$ pounder. It was fascinating to see far more swallows and other migrants had arrived than we had seen in the south of England, a pair of yellow wagtails being amongst them – probably as far north as they go. Mattie drove Aylmer down one morning to fish the Straights and, stopping to open the gate at the bottom of the hill, they disturbed a goshawk feeding on a cock pheasant it had killed and half eaten. My wife and I arrived about an hour later, and seeing a half eaten cock pheasant lying in the field but not knowing how it came to be there, I began to fish the Castle Pool, when a goshawk flew very fast right over the pool and back towards its kill. But it did not settle and went off in search of quieter pastures. I must say I viewed its presence with mixed feelings for I

love red squirrels, which are still holding out in the area – an especially lovely sight when fishing – and goshawks though rare and beautiful birds, are one of their deadly enemies. It is, of course, such episodes as these that puts the icing on an already delightful cake, for the whole stretch of river is one of unspoilt great beauty. Existing pools have in some cases been improved and the water now available covers something like four miles, double what was available when we first fished there. With many varied pools and much good fly-fishing water, there are now two extremely comfortable cottages available to cover their respective beats.

It would be wrong to close any account of the North Tyne without mentioning the splendid runs of sea trout that occur from early summer onwards. On my first ever visit I was lucky enough to catch a five pounder with almost my first cast on a Thunder and Lightning in the Castle Pool – a splendid introduction in anyone's book.

The following year a three pounder followed. As my car was close at hand I deposited it in the back and went on to complete the pool, hoping to catch another. I forgot I had left my labrador who is partial to pretty well anything edible except celery, in the car as well. When I returned a few minutes later only 1½lb of my fish was left! However, none of this can compare with a local garage owner who caught an 18½lb sea trout, spinning on a stretch of the river near Wark. I was told by Mattie that his business had gone bust and been taken over. He had apparently spent too much time fishing – but who can blame him!

*A clean-up scheme was started by the Northumbrian Water Authority in 1973 to what was then the most polluted river in Britain. Even now the Tyne still has more sewage in it than any other salmon river, and this causes an oxygen deficit in the narrow estuary waters that kills hundreds of fish in dry summers, when there is insufficient flow to cleanse it. Salmon started returning in the late 1970s and by 1988 the returns for the Tyne showed 1,000 fish being caught. In 1998 this figure has risen to 1,750 salmon despite one or two poor years, and just under 2,500 sea trout – figures published by the environment agency recently. This is still far less than recorded in the 1880s when the Chipchase beat alone caught 391 salmon in 1885, with a total weight of 3,042 lb.*

*The record salmon on the Chipchase beat of the North Tyne was caught by T.G. Taylor, the present owner's grandfather, on 7 October 1930. It was a cock fish, hooked in the Mill Stream on a number 12 double-hook Durham Ranger and weighed 42 lb – possibly the biggest salmon ever caught on the Tyne.*

*My 18½ pounder.*

OPPOSITE:
*Castle Pool with Chipchase Castle in the background.*

# The Moisie River

THE MOISIE RIVER runs into the St Lawrence a few miles east of Seven Islands. With its source in Labrador 240 miles north and fed from a vast area by numerous lakes, rivers and streams as it carves its way south through canyon and forest, it must rate as one of the truly great Atlantic salmon rivers of the world, and when it flows into the St Lawrence at Moisie village it is over a mile wide.

The drive from Seven Islands to the Moisie Salmon Club main camp through miles of spruce altogether belies the sudden and unexpected splendour of the river setting which greets your arrival opposite the main camp some fifteen miles from the sea. One moment among rather scruffy spruce, the next a sweeping panorama of water and wilderness as the river, stretching out for miles, curves out of sight amid the surrounding hills. Iced up throughout winter, it stays at a high level through melting snow, ice and spring rain until late May or early June when salmon enter the river and fresh runs continue well into July.

Dating back to well before the First World War the Moisie Salmon Club's history has been delightfully recorded by Edward Weeks in his book *The Moisie Salmon Club*. It was my great good fortune to be twice invited there many years ago by Ginny Beede, one of the members, and her husband Bob. A magical experience and one I shall never forget. As my two visits took place before high seas drift netting had begun to take its toll of Canada's east coast salmon fishing, salmon were there in abundance, but it was the setting which made such an impact, for the river was one of such awesome power and grandeur as it flowed past the main camp – or further upstream cascaded down through gorges at incredible speed – that one marvelled how salmon could somehow surmount this extraordinary force of water. Before our arrival Bob had warned me I might have to rough it – a splendid leg-pull as things turned out for their house – like those of the other members, built of local pine – couldn't have been more comfortable with a beautifully appointed living room from which on either side led our bedrooms complete with bath and electricity laid on – even ice for our Martinis!

*The Moisie River – on the way up to the Cran Serré from the Fork's Camp.*

That first evening I needed it. I had just lost three salmon in the Royal Pools close at hand, after having each one on for almost half an hour; all of them would have tipped the scales at around 20lb – some way to start! By way of consolation prize I landed a thirteen pounder which Julian, my guide, knocked on the head before I could stop him – it was a Kelt! What Canadians call Black Salmon, but apparently they were fair game then. Julian was pretty scathing about my reel which had a hopelessly inadequate check – quite useless in such heavy water – and Bob, on hearing and seeing for himself very kindly insisted on my using one of his. This had a splendid six-stop drag on it, which I used from then on and all went well. All this occurred long before disc brakes were pretty well standard.

The next morning I went up with Bob to the Island Pool where salmon encountered their first rapids after leaving the sea. A huge volume of water split round an island with a sheer rock face on one side. At one point Bob warned me that if I allowed a salmon to take me downstream and we had to follow in the canoe it would take an hour to paddle back against the current, so great was the flow. 'So make sure it's a big one if you do it' were his famous last words – it was too, but we unfortunately parted company first! A simple hut had been erected on the island to give shelter when needed to a couple of Indians of the Montaignais tribe, armed with ancient rifles, who were stationed there to shoot seals that had followed the salmon in from the sea. Not being marvellous shots they scared their quarry more often than not, which hopefully had the desired effect!

There had been a colossal flood up north a few days earlier which had delayed our own arrival, but the Island Pools were already full of salmon waiting to ascend the rapids. A few days later it was to give me one of the best morning's fishing of my life with four large salmon all caught on a size six shrimp fly before the skies darkened, the fish went off the take as a thunderstorm put paid to proceedings. No carbon graphite rods to worry about then! It was a fascinating experience, for as the skies darkened the air filled with nighthawks – a close relative of our nightjar – and their aerial manoeuvres as they caught their insect dinner ahead of time was a joy to watch.

The rapids at the Island Pools marked the top limit of river owned by the Club. Opposite the main camp, and both above and below it, within relatively easy paddling distance lay a number of pools where the river was a good two hundred yards wide. Perhaps the most famous were the Royal

OPPOSITE:
*The view of the main camp on arrival.*

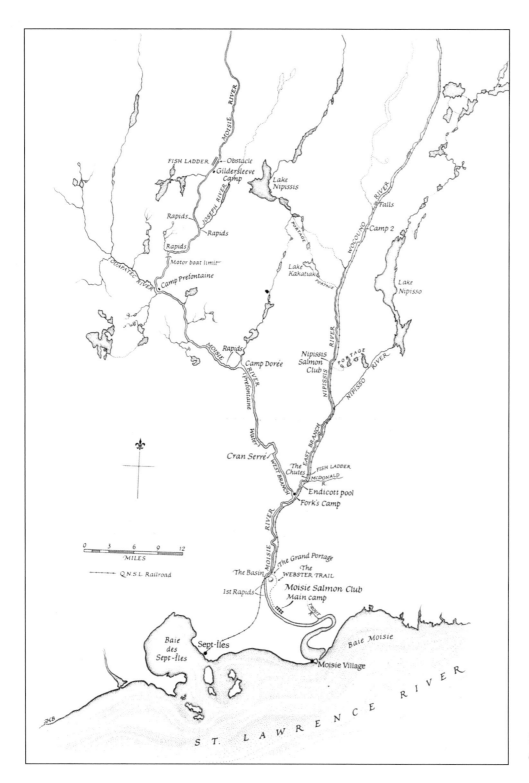

*The Moisie River, Province of Quebec.*

Pools, right opposite the main camp. Taking our position from markers on each bank we anchored, cast either side of our canoe, then upped anchor to drop down a few yards and anchored again to cover the next bit and so on. One afternoon doing just this, I hooked a beauty which proceeded to rip off line and backing non-stop and there was just no holding it. The normal procedure then was quite simple – up anchor and either make for the shore or if necessary follow. On this occasion the anchor refused to budge despite the most frantic efforts of my guide. By the time I had produced a knife to cut the rope it was all over!

Recounting this to Bob he told me of one occasion when anchored like-wise he suddenly saw in the evening light what he took to be a huge log bearing down on them in the swift current. Before they could clear the anchor his 'log' swept past, narrowly missing their canoe, and clambered out on to the bank below before disappearing into the forest – his 'log' had turned into a bull moose!

On my second trip we flew upstream by floatplane to fish the east and west branches from the Fork's Camp. Before alighting our pilot suggested we

*Take off by floatplane from the main camp.*

*The Cran Serré from our Cessna floatplane.*

might like to look down on our pools from the air, and at about a thousand feet he flew us over the Chutes of the east branch and Cran Serré of the west, beat headwaters of their respective branches. Little did I realise then as we gazed down just what marvellous fishing we were to experience. In the next three days my hostess and I caught some forty-five salmon, and of those kept (the limit then was six a day) we averaged just fractionally under 20lb a fish. But if the fishing was superlative the setting was more so. The Fork's Camp itself, a trifle more primitive than its main counterpart, had more than a touch of backwood's atmosphere about it, with its mixture of log cabins, tents, a snow house for keeping fish fresh and ice cool, and kerosene for lighting. Ideally positioned, it offered immediate access to east and west branches at their junction with the main river. Here the canoes were built to accommodate an outboard motor, for the current was so swift

OPPOSITE:
*The Chutes – a roaring torrent of tremendous power, cascading down through the gorge.*

*Ginny's 30lber – an extremly long fish. Had it been deeper we all thought it would have scaled 40lb.*

OPPOSITE:
*Ginny Beede playing a salmon at Palmer Pool, Cran Serré.*

that it was impossible to paddle upstream against it even by hugging the bank.

On my first visit a few years earlier we fished the east branch first, where it becomes the Nipissis River above the Chutes. We went ashore before lunch below the Chutes, walking upstream along a trail through woods carpeted with Canadian dogwood, a dwarf, creeping, star-shaped, flowering plant which at dusk and in the dark became almost luminous and *en masse* presented an unbelievably beautiful sight. Here and there wild orchids enriched the path and paper bark birch, their fresh green leaves and vivid white trunks glistening in the sunlight, interspersed with the darker green of young spruce, created an unforgettable picture. The trail followed down to the river but so dense were the trees that we could only catch a brief glimpse here and there of the ever faster running water. As we drew closer to the Chutes the thunder of water increased until suddenly we came in sight of the rapids. And what a sight it was – a roaring torrent of tremendous power cascading down through the gorge, which funnelled the stream into a golden foaming frenzy, with added force from the MacDonald River that slammed into it at right angles from the opposite bank. Some hundred yards below it levelled out into an extremely fast running and turbulent pool where salmon rest prior to attempting the ascent. After several days of flood the river was still too high to make this possible, but as the water dropped, rock ledges, flattened over the years by the tremendous and constant force of water, enabled the salmon to screen themselves partially from the main current. By working up under these ledges when water height allowed, they would rest there, then jump upwards through the mad rush of water in a desperate leap to reach the sanctuary of the ledge above – and so on until they reached the calmer waters.

We returned to our canoes and fished till lunch below the rapids, but few salmon had as yet managed the long journey upstream and we had no luck. Shooting downstream, the current increasing our outboard's momentum to speed boat proportions, we fished the pools at the junction of the

*Salmon resuscitation: 'holding an exhausted salmon by the tail, our guide would draw it gently back and forth to force water through its gills'.*

fork. About teatime – in time only! – Ginny hooked a beauty. Bob and I were sharing a canoe some fifty yards from her, and as he had just risen a salmon, he concentrated on trying to catch it while I gave him a running commentary on her progress. As the minutes ticked by we realised this was no small fish. Half an hour went by and then an hour. The salmon had long since decided it wanted to return to the sea and we had visions of sending the floatplane so that Ginny could be back in time for supper. She was only just in sight when, by the evening sun, I caught sight of a silvery flash as the net lifted a magnificent salmon safely out of the water. It had taken one hour and ten minutes to land and weighed exactly 30lb. As the photograph shows it was an extremely long fish – had it been deeper we all thought it would have scaled 40lb. After supper the sun set on a world of utter peace and tranquillity as we stood outside watching the magic of the northern lights flicking silvery rays skyward into a star-filled heaven. It was the perfect ending to a wonderful day.

The next day we all fished the pools at the Cran Serré – without doubt so far as I was concerned the most spectacular setting of any pool on any river I have ever fished. To get there from the Fork Camp was itself a remarkable experience, for transportation upstream against a heavy current necessitated the use of a large flat-bottomed canoe with very powerful outboard, and even then progress was not rapid.

On leaving the Fork's Camp the river banks, covered with birch and spruce and dotted with dwarf moose maple, rise at first gently on either side, later giving way to steeper and, in places, precipitous rock outcrops. The river narrows, funnelling the current into turbulence not unlike a kettle about to boil, then opening out at the Cran into a huge bowl set amid the surrounding hills, edged by sheer rock that rises several hundred feet to north and north-east. A shingle-covered island forms the centre-piece, splitting the rapids above into two streams where salmon rest before moving on. On our way upstream we saw a moose calf feeding by the water's edge, and as we planed in at high speed for a closer look he remained amazingly unconcerned until we were quite close. We saw kingfishers – large birds, about the size of our jay but lacking the vivid colouring of our European kingfisher – and just before reaching the island my guide pointing upwards to the top of a spruce said 'porc-epic' – porcupine!

We proceeded to have wonderful sport, and might have exceeded our limit shortly after lunch had we not released several smaller fish. Anything less than 15/16lb went back immediately. After a hard fight some salmon needed a little assistance or they would have floated away, belly up, with no chance of survival. Holding an exhausted salmon by the tail, our guide would draw it gently back and forth to force water through its gills. This

*Ted Bates in action – playing a salmon from the canoe.*

worked wonders and in no time it would be on its way, none the worse for the encounter. Ted Bates, who I will mention again later, told me that, in a previous year, having reached his limit of six for the day, he released three salmon he was sure were each over 30lb – some fishing! All this took place over thirty years ago when catch and release had hardly been heard of here.

In hot weather the guides often left any salmon caught and killed, in the river to keep them cool, tethering them with nylon to the branch of a bush or heavy stone. One day on doing just this Ginny and her guides returned to collect their catch to find a mink in possession. It stood its ground, chattering at them in rage and fury at being disturbed in its meal, before being driven off by the guides, armed with a canoe paddle – an event one or two of us have experienced here since mink are, unfortunately, now part of the scene on so many British rivers.

The next morning Ginny decided to fish the east branch below the Chutes. As she and her Indian guides rounded a bend on their way upstream they saw an animal, riding high in the water, swimming across the river; it turned out to be a lynx. This was too much for the Indians to resist; they gave chase, fully intending to capture it, but nearly succeeded in capsizing the canoe in the process before the lynx made good its escape. The episode, fortunately, did nothing to impair Ginny's fishing prowess, and she joined us for lunch – minus fur – but with two salmon each of over 20lb.

Almost every season several salmon of over 30lb are caught and quite often one or more of over 40lb. For beginners luck Ginny's niece, Virginia, must surely take the prize. Fishing for the first time in her life, aged 19, I believe, on one of the Royal Pools, in a canoe with her father, she cast her fly out close to the canoe; it was promptly seized by a salmon. After a two-hour battle, aided and abetted in no small way by her father, it was finally netted. It weighed 40$\frac{1}{4}$lb!

But what is a giant on the Moisie? To answer this I am indebted to Ted Bates, a long time Moisie member, for his description of a colossal salmon he hooked in the Palmer Pool at the Cran, as set out so splendidly in Edward Week's book – and I quote – 'What is a giant? It is a salmon that weighs at least 50lb and might even beat the world's hook and line record which at present stands at 79lb. That super giant was taken on a spoon in the Aaro River in Northern Norway'. Such fish in the Moisie? Well let's see, . . . Some years ago a phone call came in to the Moisie Camp to Mitchell Campbell (the camp superintendent). He was startled to hear the man at the commercial weighing-in station in Sept Îles announce that a netter had just sold him four giant fish. These fish had been weighed together. The four tipped the scales at 230lb. . . When Mitch got there they had been cleaned. Not much could be proved by weighing cleaned fish. However, two were very much larger fish – super giants in fact. The other two – though smaller – were still big enough to scare you! If two super giants weighed 60lb apiece which seems a reasonable assumption, the tiny ones must have weighed 55lb apiece.

In 1964 what happened to you on any cast happened to me. This adventure turned out so sadly that I think it made two Indians cry. I'd gone up to the Cran Serré with my eighty-year-old gaffer Francois Jerome and his phlegmatic son, Donald, one morning to try the Palmer Pool. I fastened a size 8 Jock Scott on a seven-pound leader and flipped it out into the current. Donald was already asleep.

But when something frightening came out of there with a smash, took the Jock Scott, ran across the pool and leaped once, making a sound like a glacier calving, Donald woke up! Francois who doesn't often say anything said '*Soixante livres*'. I looked again at the next jump and agreed with him. The salmon was a giant – maybe not sixty pounds – but so close to it that caution seized us in its jittery grasp. We handled that fish like it was our last

*Bob Beede fishing the Palmer Pool. Without doubt, so far as I was concerned, the most spectacular setting of any pool on any river I have fished.*

act in a very long life. We worked our way down around the bar with the water-rounded stones on it ever so slowly. Finding that we couldn't do anything with him in the hole, which swirls around below, we eased him gradually over to the far bank where the old camp used to stand. At that point he was pretty tired and ready for the net. But he was just too big to move.

As we followed his drift down past the location of the camp, the fish was always in full view. He looked to be at least twice as big as any fish that I'd ever seen and the view was good. Most of the time he wallowed two or three feet beyond the reach of Donald who, if nothing else, is the best man with the net I ever saw. Donald was wide-awake this time too! But the great salmon's weight and the current there made it impossible to swing him – even an inch – let alone those vital couple of feet.

We kept backing down and backing down. Finally we passed the point of no return and it was obvious that the rapids were almost upon us. There was nothing we could do except put a little more strain, hoping that a current or eddy would help us bring him in the two or three feet that would put his head in the net. As we approached the rapids, I put that bit of extra pressure on the fish from a point on the bank that looked to be advantageous. But I knew all the time, having seen the well-frayed leader clearly for half an hour, that success was not to be our reward.

The salmon's head turned a little. I thought perhaps I was wrong and he was coming. But that giant tail gave a now feeble wag and that was that. Donald who is not famous for his energy went right into the water waist deep, then to his shoulders and flailed madly about like an Indian with a quart of whiskey in him, trying to get the net under the salmon. But the fish just dropped back with the current, half on its belly, half on its side. Donald never reached him. Ashore he struggled, wet and bedraggled, and sat down beside Francois and me. I looked at the two Indians. Nobody said a word.

Of course, it could have been the spray from that flailing net but I swear I saw moisture coming out of those Indian eyes. They both stared at the water. They stared at where the fish had sunk slowly out of sight. They stared at me. Francois finally said – once again – *Soixante livres*, and then they turned their backs and walked up the river toward the spot where we had left the canoe.

A wonderful account and truly fascinating story.

Many billions of gallons of water have flowed into the St Lawrence since I was last fishing the Moisie, and I had lost touch as both Bob and Ginny, my host and hostess, died years ago. The Moisie, in common with all Canadian East Coast rivers, has suffered from the effects of drift net fishing until its banning; from iron ore pollution to the Nipissis, which for a time badly affected the spawning grounds of the east branch, and from a major oil spill from a derailment that occurred on the track that takes vast tons of iron ore from the Knob Lake area in Labrador to Sept Îles. This spillage was purged fortunately by a monumental flood, that at the same time completely covered and washed away the Fork's Camp, now rebuilt.

Recently, however, I made welcome contact with Mitchell Campbell who was camp superintendent when I was there. Apart from his war service in the Canadian Navy he was employed by the Moisie Salmon Club before the war and for many years after. He has retired as camp superintendent but was retained as a consultant, and elected a member of the Board of Directors each year, and is now Executive Assistant to the President. It is fair to say that what he doesn't know about the Moisie isn't worth knowing. His recent letter to me gives up-to-date news that the salmon run is down perhaps $12\frac{1}{2}$ per cent. That is, on what it was when I was last there in 1965 – some achievement compared to the desperate straits of most of our salmon rivers. More encouraging still, the plans they have for the Moisie are upbeat, with stock eventually exceeding that which I experienced, and which he feels will provide great sport for many generations to come. A wonderful outlook.

\* \* \* \* \* \* \* \* \*

*For fishermen with a scientific turn of mind the following will be of interest. Research carried out after the First World War and since, by the examination of scales from a large number of salmon, has revealed some fascinating facts about the Moisie salmon. The first is that a much larger than usual number returned to spawn a second, and even a third time, cock fish included. With the co-operation of Jock Menzies, the famous Scottish marine biologist who visited the Moisie on two occasions, scales from one thousand five hundred and eighty-five salmon were sent from the Moisie to be read under the microscope over a five-year period. The number of salmon that survived to return to the Moisie for a third and fourth time was of a far higher ratio than occurred in Scotland, and one salmon of 32lb had spawned four times and was on its way upstream to a fifth spawning when caught.*

*Perhaps this accounts in no small way for the remarkable average weight of around 20lb.*

# The Helmsdale

IT HAS BEEN MY GOOD FORTUNE, as a guest of great friend Gerald Moyers, to fish the Helmsdale for something like fourteen consecutive years. Mention the Helmsdale to anyone who has fished there and their faces light up at the very thought of all it offers, for it is the gem of a river.

From Loch Achnamoine to the sea – some 26 miles – the river flows first through open moorland with grouse, deer and adders – I nearly hooked one once as it was swimming across one of the top pools – then more fertile farmland for the remainder of the Strath. It is all good sheep country, with an abundance of wildlife.

Before my first visit we received an invitation to supper with friends who wanted me to meet someone who had fished there for over forty years. After supper I asked him what flies he recommended. 'Ah' he said 'I thought you'd ask me that', and putting his hand in his pocket extracted an envelope with three small flies he had tied himself. 'If you show these to Johnnie MacDonald (our ghillie to be) he will know who tied them!'

He also gave me an introduction to a lifelong friend, who I will simply call Jim, who happened to be staying in Helmsdale when we were there and who also knew every inch of the river like the back of his hand. Little did I realise at the time that this twin action was to lead to one of the most enjoyable evening's fishing I have ever had.

We arrived on a Sunday in what the weather forecasters would describe as unsettled weather. But our already high spirits rose considerably when my host, who had come up the week before, told us of all the fish they had caught and that there seemed plenty more in the river! Monday came with high, squally winds and plenty of cloud, and we returned to our hotel in the evening with six fish – a wonderful introduction to the river. Our first impressions were only slightly marred on hearing the weather forecast of an anticyclone over north-east Scotland, with sun and little cloud – and so it proved, for the next four days would have done credit to the Mediterranean! In fact, most of us had given up hope of catching any salmon

*Loch Achnamoine (local 'Namoine), from which the Helmsdale flows.*

during the day and had either woken early to fish before breakfast or taken our time over supper before chancing our flies in the gloaming which, by mid-June in the north of Scotland, seemed to extend almost throughout the night.

By Friday afternoon, with still no cloud in sight and only one day's fishing left before our return south, I asked my host, if he wasn't going to fish after supper, if I might ask Jim to come with me, for we had only two rods per beat. Although staying in our hotel, he had been fishing the Brora but, without rain, it was only a trickle and therefore virtually useless. We took our time over supper, leaving the hotel around 8.30pm for one of the upper beats some fifteen miles upstream. The sun was still high and bright, and we had driven about three miles when Jim drew into a lay-by above the river. 'We'll just stop here for a moment and have a few quick casts into the run at the head of this pool.' said my companion, 'The hill behind screens it from the sun earlier than the upper pools and it is always possible that a fresh salmon has moved up into roughish water by this time of the evening.'

Clambering down a steepish bank, we waded almost half-way across and immediately above to where a shallow ledge formed a lie in the white water. As instructed, I cast at only a slight angle to allow my fly – one of the specials I had been given – to come round and hang straight downstream.

A few quick casts Jim had said, and there cannot have been many more than a dozen when the water erupted and line tore off my reel as a beautiful silver fresh salmon shot down, across and four feet out of the water about 20 yards from where he'd taken.

'What a beauty,' I exclaimed as it made off again. 'Yes, about 8 lb,' came the reply. 'I think it's a bit bigger than that,' I muttered, as more line screeched off the reel.

With 20 or 30 yards of backing out, in next to no time it made another spectacular leap – 'Yes, about 15 lb,' my companion agreed.

Suffice it to say, that for the next few minutes I was led a most exciting dance all over the pool until eventually the fish began to tire and very slowly, and with considerable difficulty, for it was an extremely strong fish, I inched it nearer and nearer. The lowering sun's rays, though screened by the hill, produced an opaque glare on the water, making vision extremely difficult beneath its surface – even Polaroids were of little help. Jim, who had my big net, declared firmly that he couldn't see to net it, and that I'd better gaff it myself. 'Which hand do you like your gaff in?' 'My left,' I said without thinking and, to this day, I can't think why for I have never ever gaffed a fish with my left hand! The fight was still by no means over, as the salmon was taking a very poor view of being brought into shallower water and was still amazingly fresh. Perhaps worrying because I was taking too long and so stopping us both fishing higher up, I made a futile dab at it, knowing as I did so that it was just out of reach. I only succeeded in catching my line! New life surged into my fish as it stripped off fresh yards of line – which fortunately slipped freely round the gaff – and after what seemed an eternity, and helped by Jim, I once more made proper contact. I think that salmon put up one of the toughest fights of any I have caught since fishing in Canada, and it was not until he had tired completely that I was able to gaff him as he came within reach. This time I made no mistake. Only as I lifted him out of the water did we both, I think, realise why he had

*Fishing the Douarst Pool, River Helmsdale with a 12ft 6in carbon graphite rod.*

fought so hard and long, for his girth was prodigious. It was a marvellous start to the evening and Jim was, if anything, more delighted than I was.

Driving up the strath on a glorious June evening added a further dimension of enjoyment, for at that time of year it is teeming with wildlife of all descriptions. By then, many summer migrants are busy rearing their young – wheatear, ringed plover, curlew, oyster catchers and lapwings abound and we even saw one or two families of greylags. As dusk descended, rabbits came out in their hundreds. On either side of the river sheep and well-grown lambs added an extra air of plenty and well-being as we drove on upstream.

The upper reaches of our beat were of an entirely different character, being much narrower, shallower pools that flowed in almost meandering fashion through moorland heather and grass. Two salmon had been

*Living up to its name – a lapwing circles overhead. Its young must be near.*

*Looking up Strath Helmsdale from the Marrel.*

*Two of the three before-lunch salmon – with two rather bored looking Labradors!*

caught there during the morning in bright sunlight and we had been told one pool in particular was full of fish. The drive there took roughly 15 minutes, but before making our way to what was considered the best pool of all, I was given a detailed run-down of another pool – the red brae – that Jim thought worth trying. He insisted on coming down with me and showed me exactly where to start and where I might rise a salmon, saying he would fish one pool not far above whilst I tried there, and come back for me before returning to the car. Left on my own, I had barely covered a third of the pool when a good fish took my fly, exactly where I had been told, and in reasonable time I had him on the bank just as Jim returned to pick me up. I could not help reflecting what a bonus it was to be with someone who

*Success at last!*

knew the river so intimately. To the uninitiated so much water looks fishable and so much time can be wasted that the real opportunity is often missed.

We moved on upstream and came to the pool that had been so successful earlier in the day. I did my best to persuade Jim to fish it down but he declined, saying he never had much luck there, and fished the pool immediately below. Mine looked absolutely perfect and with every cast I expected a rise and that exhilarating tug of contact but, despite fishing most carefully, neither of us moved a thing. The light was by then fading though, at 11pm, still light enough to read by as we walked down to try two last pools. I was again well briefed by Jim and again I was lucky enough to hook a good fish almost at the head of the pool which played well, fighting mostly upstream so that the lower water was not disturbed. I was fortunate enough to land it in less than ten minutes.

It was an interesting reflection that, with little light left, it had been as easy to see to gaff this salmon as the first one had been difficult. Jim's delight on his return to see my third salmon lying in the heather was most heart-warming, but it had been entirely thanks to him that I had managed to catch any salmon at all. I was as glad for his sake as mine that I had not let him down.

I had used the special fly I had been given on and off ever since I had arrived five days earlier without moving a single fish, although I had caught two and lost one the first day, one on a Thunder and one on a Canadian fly that went by the romantic name of Moonlight. In fact, I must confess I was beginning to have some doubts about my present until that evening.

I persuaded Jim to use my rod and fly over the rest of the pool which had not been disturbed. But although he rose a salmon well down the pool, it never touched the fly and wouldn't come again.

On our return to the hotel around midnight I made my way to the larder with my three salmon and found scales with which to weigh them. They registered 14, 14 and 22 lb. At this point, our hotel proprietor arrived, himself a keen angler, and seeing what I had just done said that if I had been using his scales they weighed a pound light. Surely the perfect answer to the Angler's Prayer!

*Stags in velvet pause for a drink before crossing.*

# Steelhead adventure

**I**F YOU ARE A FISHERMAN with a sense of adventure, love real wilderness and all that goes with it, then undoubtedly a trip to the far north of British Columbia to fish for steelhead is something you will never forget. But don't expect to be coddled – wading up to your middle in ice cold water is not everyone's cup of tea, whilst the grizzly round the next bend, might make a dash to the boat a sensible precaution – yes, it actually happened to two of our party, though the photograph of the event proved somewhat shaky!

Five of us had flown from London and New York to meet up at Vancouver before flying the next morning to Prince George, some 300 miles further north – a spectacularly beautiful early morning flight over the sunlit Coast Mountains. At Prince George we were joined by a delightful American, Fred H, the only member of our party who knew what was in store. He had fished the River Sustut on more than one occasion and his description of huge steelheads and past exploits fired our enthusiasm still further.

One-and-a-half hours after take-off and after flying through mountain passes for the latter part of our flight, we touched down on a gravel landing strip cut through the forest overlooking Bear River. It had been a fascinating experience to see the country below us streaked with lakes and rivers, and carpeted with a patchwork of spruce, poplar and cottonwood in vivid autumn gold and orange. A herd of mountain goats in the hill face just before landing made an unforgettable picture.

A short wait at Bear River for our helicopter which, piloted by a Canadian nicknamed Radar, ferried us the last eight miles to Suskeena Lodge – but not before we had time to see a family of bald eagles fly up from Bear River below us. They had been feeding on dead and dying sockeye and king salmon which spawn there.

Radar had ferried the previous weeks guests in for the changeover. They had had a splendid weeks fishing and we were given some helpful tips by one of the party who warned us that if we weren't catching the bottom with every other cast we weren't fishing deep enough! Doug Robertson, our host for the next ten days and owner of Suskeena, greeted us warmly, along with his three splendid guides, Emil, Floyd and Phil, and made us feel

OPPOSITE:
*Bear River, with Motase Peak (7,956ft) in the background.*

83

at home in no time at all. Floyd's wife, Wendy, cooked superbly for us all, with her assistant, Marla, and the steelhead and moose, which most of us had never tasted before, were out of this world. In fact we were incredibly well looked after, and but for much wading and casting, would have put on pounds! The camp, with a large log cabin where we all ate and relaxed, had been set up some ten to eleven years earlier in a near perfect setting over-looking the Sustut River, with mountains rising to 7,500 to 8,000 ft around.

We unpacked, lunched, and shortly after 2.00 pm were ready for the fray. After a dry September the water was at a very low level and absolutely gin clear, and I was just beginning to think there were no steelhead around when my fly – which went by the inelegant name of Black Bastard – was seized in the most dramatic fashion and for the next fifteen minutes I was on the receiving end of one of the finest fighting performances, with three spectacular running leaps upstream, that I have ever had the good fortune to experience. After much heart searching and many anxious moments, it was finally beached and, being a hen fish – of around 10 to 11 lb – we released her unharmed. She certainly deserved to be!

*Emil with my first steelhead – a female around 10 lb, which we released.*

*Flying over the coastal
mountains on our way to
the River Sustut from
Vancouver.*

*A beaver's dam quite close to the main river.*

That I had been incredibly lucky so early on was beyond question, for no one else caught a steelhead that afternoon. As the days progressed it really was a question of quality rather than quantity, for we must have averaged around 12 to 14 lb a fish.

For five of us it was a totally new and quite enthralling experience. Wherever we wandered along the banks of the river, or as on one occasion were taken by Floyd, our guide, to see a beaver's dam, tracks of moose, grizzlies, wolf, mink and other animals were everywhere. Bald and golden eagles – especially the former which had nested in a cottonwood tree by one of our pools – were an everyday occurrence. Being early October, all summer migrants had already left – hard frosts at night and snow high up providing a sufficient warning to them that 'Fall' was well and truly under way.

Water temperature around 37°F made wading out at the end of a 'run' a welcome relief; in such conditions the steelhead lay very close to the bottom. Quick sinking lines were the order of the day, a type of fly-fishing for which some of us were poorly equipped. Thanks to Fred's generosity, my son and I were provided with the necessary quick sinking shooting heads and picked up the technique of covering the fast flowing wide pools adequately. But it was Fred himself, who, on the only day we all lunched together round a campfire (Fred never ate lunch or breakfast) put on a superb display for us all. A superlative caster, he continued fishing whilst we sat around with mugs of steaming soup to warm us, and hooked what for a moment we all thought was a relatively small fish. We were soon to realize how wrong we were as a magnificent male steelhead suddenly went wild, jumped to show us his size and then tore line off Fred's reel as it

*Wolf tracks (left) and grizzly tracks (right).*

*The moment of triumph. Fred clasps his magnificent male steelhead to his chest.*

streaked across to the other side of the river. With almost 100 yards of line and backing out, rocks in the shallow water near the far bank became an agonising hazard. But gradually, yard by yard, with tremendous strain on such a long line, Fred coaxed his fish back to safety and, after what seemed hours, eventually beached it. Quickly removing the fly, a simple job, for he always fished without a barb, he whipped his handkerchief round its tail and clasped it to his chest for us to photograph. Then he very gently returned it to the water, making certain it had fully recovered, and released it to continue its journey upstream. From leaving the sea it had already navigated 400 miles of fast flowing river and would, we were told, journey another 50 before spawning. It must have weighed well over 20 lb – the largest steelhead that any of us caught. His encounter was committed to both cinefilm and still photographs by all of us present and now makes a fitting record of his success. Fred never fishes with a barb and never kills his fish – action we might well follow, even if limited to the release of hen (Atlantic) salmon, in view of the crisis which surrounds their survival.

*Gradually, yard by yard, Fred coaxed his fish back to safety from the rocks on the far side.*

Our nine days were full of so many delightful episodes – even the catching of a Dolly Varden, a type of char, was fun, though usually they were gratefully removed from the river and left on the bank for bears and other animals.

Each evening, as we were all seated round a log fire, our host Doug Robertson would ask us what sort of a day we'd had and record it all on tape. On one particularly wet day – the only one we had in fact – as we were walking back to our cabin after supper Aylmer turned to me with a half smile and said 'we didn't have our commercial today!' Our one horrible day was not for recording! I had thought his tape was to be sent to his wife in New York to give her a picture of what was going on, but to my surprise and delight I was made a present of it by Doug. He had christened one of the long pools 'Robin's run' in memory of a great day and where I lost my big fish. On playing it at home my youngest son Tom said 'let's see what's on the other side' and we proceeded to be serenaded by the most marvellous tenor, singing all the old favourites like *Smoke gets in your Eyes*, *The Way you Look Tonight* and so on – and they were sung superbly. I sent a copy of the tape to Doug, who wrote back, not having realised there was anything on the reverse side, to say 'the selections were sung by John Davidson, a deep-sea diver, who took up singing; his lungs were well developed with his work. Alas, money and success went to his head and he started drinking and carousing about, losing his wife and two boys as well as his voice and I have not heard much about the rest of his life. I only met him in L.A. once – he seemed a great guy.' Maybe he should have taken up fishing!

We had hoped to get Radar one afternoon to fly us up above the tree line to see the caribou herds with which he had been intimately concerned. But, alas, it was not to be, as the weather closed in on the only chance we had. By way of compensation he flew us to see and fish the junction pool where the Sustut flowed into the Skeena, with spectacular views of the forest and mountain pass. With no luck there we helicoptered upstream a few miles and landed by a long pool, where we all fished. Radar put up his telescopic spinning rod – a most useful gadget to fly around with in a small helicopter – and, armed with a large spoon and barbless hook, was soon into a big male steelhead that gave him a splendid fight before he finally beached it. It weighed 16 lb – a prize he had more than earned through his kindness to us all.

If I was fortunate in catching the first fish, the same comment applied almost in reverse – but with a different ending! Having fished all day with-

*Radar with his 16lb steelhead (top). Unloading the helicopter (bottom).*

out success, Floyd, while manoeuvring the boat in much shallower water, spotted two or three steelhead I felt sure we must have frightened, but we anchored nonetheless for a last chance. Almost first cast I felt as if I'd caught the bottom, struck and from then on for the next ten minutes it seemed the world stopped still. With anchor up, Floyd made for the shore and, just as the boat touched bottom, my fish made the most spectacular running jump about three feet out of the water in mid-stream, all 28 to 30 lb of it – the most enormous steelhead I had ever seen with a beautiful crimson band down his immensely deep side. Neither Floyd, who was looking after the boat, or Aylmer, who was struggling to unzip his cine camera, actually saw it jump – to my very great regret – only the tidal wave it made on re-entry! It was a sight I shall always remember. It then proceeded to take about 120 yards of line and backing across and downstream, and there was just nothing I could do to stop it. We parted company under considerable strain but, on reeling in for what seemed an age, the fly came back with an extremely large scale embedded on it – it had been foul hooked! Had the hold held I believe I'd still be playing it!

I really didn't mind losing it, but I would love to have known its exact weight. Of course it will be bigger next year and bigger still the year after – and, as I reflected that last evening, if I had landed him I'd have been terribly overweight on the flight home!

# A weekend at
# The Snows, Lake Huron

ARRIVING ONE EARLY OCTOBER AFTERNOON some years ago at Sault Ste Marie airport on the Michigan Ontario border, my wife and I were met by great American friends, Ruth and Len Smith, who had known me since I was a boy. They had invited us for a long weekend to their summer house, The Snows, beautifully situated on a small island in Lake Huron. We were both really looking forward to it, especially after a very hectic two weeks of business; a moment or two of relaxation was just what the doctor ordered. Any idea of relaxing, however, were soon dispelled – for me at least – when Len announced that the 'fall' duck migration should be in full swing, and their area of Lake Huron was plumb in the middle of the central flyway.

A 5 am start was the order of the day. I think we eventually settled for 5.30! By the time we had loaded the decoys into his Chriscraft and had a quick cup of coffee it was nearer 6 am, but still dark, as we left his boathouse and moved out into the lake. Fifteen minutes later Len brought

*Len Smith in his Chriscraft,*
*preparing to fish Lake Huron.*

93

the Chriscraft into a sheltered bay, where we put out the decoys and waited for the dawn. We waited patiently as it got lighter, and as so often happens on a morning flight, we waited and waited and no duck came anywhere near us. We saw one or two small flights in the distance, heard, I think, two or three shots from one or two other early morning enthusiasts, and that was all. We guessed the weather was still too good to bring them down from the north. We must have disturbed a beaver at work when we landed, for a fair-sized aspen had been targeted by one, with amazingly large chips lying at its base – itself a fascinating sight. I don't know how long we waited but by the time we returned we both had ravenous appetites and did justice to a marvellous breakfast of eggs, bacon, sausages, waffles and maple syrup!

Len was most disappointed, as any host would be – 'tomorrow, we'll try again and I think get up a little later!' Alas, exactly the same thing happened, neither of us fired a shot. I gathered that the surface of Lake Huron when the migration is in full swing is covered with thousands of duck, so many in fact you can hardly see the water!

The second day we went fishing on Lake Huron and this proved far more productive. Using the Chriscraft with two rods out on either side, and using very small minnows, Ruth hooked and lost a large northern pike which broke her, but we caught quite a few perch, which were put in a keep-net hanging over the side. I was slightly puzzled by this and in my innocence asked Ruth what they were going to do with them all, as, whenever we have on the rare occasion caught them in the Highlands, we have thrown them away. 'Why, we're having them for lunch' she said! And they were quite delicious, filleted and fried in butter – *perche meunière*. As sweet and nutty a dish as you could want. When we caught some the next year in the Highlands we had them cooked the same way. The same fish caught in cold clear water – but they weren't a patch on our Lake Huron ones. We blamed the cook – who else! No weekend account would be complete without reference to a notice at the entrance to the Smith's drive which read:

*Trespassers will be persecuted to the extent of one mongrel dog that ain't over sociable to strangers. Darned if I ain't fed up with this hell raising on my place!*

We had been warned! But it really wasn't the dog we worried about so much as black bears. 'Mind you don't step on one' Len had said to me as

*Beaver's work – almost caught in the act!*

we were strolling through the wood – a mixture of spruce and aspen – in search of ruffed grouse the next morning. 'They become a bit sleepy at this time of year!' But we saw no black bears. Instead we were scolded by beautiful little pine squirrels – very much like our red squirrel – and saw a flock of evening grosbeaks feeding in the spruce trees, but the ruffed grouse were much too clever for us. It was pretty rough walking and the odds were on the grouse every time as they rose with a whirr and put themselves out of sight and harm by flying behind the nearest tree just like a woodcock. A black bear had, in fact, raided their apple tree a day or two before our arrival, and the previous winter one had broken into their neighbour's larder. When they returned in the spring to open up their house they found the place an absolute shambles – smashed cans of food lying all over the floor as the bear had sampled one tin after another and torn the place apart before getting out. Living in Britain has its advantages!

# Alaskan interlude

I F YOU WANT TO SEE MORE SALMON, albeit Pacific ones, in a day than you have probably seen in all your life, then fly to Alaska for an experience you will never forget. That is exactly what my eldest son Anthony and I did recently, though we had no idea we would witness such a sight on our first full day's fishing.

And if you can spare the time to visit one of the Nature Reserves, so much the better. By taking an extra two days we were able to include an early morning tour of the Denali National Park – itself worth going thousands of miles to see. The Park, originally two million acres and named McKinley, was extended in 1980 to six million, and renamed Denali, meaning in Athabaskan Indian 'the great one'. It comprises a tundra ecosystem that has been preserved for all time in pristine wilderness. One road only runs 85 miles through it roughly east/west, and on this access is limited to tour or shuttle buses – no private cars are allowed. Comprising an area slightly larger than the state of Massachusetts, its vastness is almost overpowering, and to cap it all the splendour of Mt McKinley at 20,320ft the highest mountain on the North American Continent. Often shrouded in cloud, we were incredibly lucky to see its snow covered sides and top on a day that dawned with sparkling clarity. In our seven hour tour, starting at 6 am, we saw moose, caribou, Dall sheep and no less than six grizzlies, one with two cubs, and scenery of quite awesome proportions.

It was a fabulous way to start our trip. We returned overnight to Anchorage, before flying to Dillingham the next morning, an hour by jet to the famed Bristol Bay area, south-west of Anchorage, where we had booked in for a week's fly fishing at the Royal Coachman Lodge.

From Dillingham a 50-minute flight by float plane, in itself a unique experience, took us over lakes and forest to the main camp ideally situated on the banks of the river Nuyakuk, which runs out of Lake Tikchik. The Lodge itself had everything anyone could possibly ask for – even a corner splendidly equipped to tie your flies – and I must add, a delightful staff to assist in any and every respect. There, according to season, you can catch

*Mount McKinley, at 20,320ft the highest mountain on the North American continent.*

all five species of Pacific salmon, wild rainbow, Arctic grayling and Arctic char; in the first week of August, we caught four of these five salmon species fishing fly only. Bill Martin and his delightful wife Mary, who own the Royal Coachman Lodge also operate an Out-Camp on the Pacific at Yantarni Bay. Due to a last minute cancellation we were offered the chance to go there, necessitating two flights, the first back to Dillingham by float plane, thence by Cessna with fixed wheels across Bristol Bay – where below us I saw my first gyr falcon and on our way back a sea otter. Then over the Aleutian Mountains, passing very close to a still active volcano, Mount Chiginagak, 6,995 ft, where steam was pouring through a fissure in its snow covered side, like some giant kettle on the boil.

We finally landed on a gravel air strip, constructed by an oil exploration company but vacated when their drilling yielded only dry wells – an ideal position for the Camp alongside the Pacific.

This Out-Camp was run by John Hickey, a one-time professor turned, in his one words, fishing buff – and a more delightful companion it would be hard to find – plus Ruby, the camp cook, who lived up to her name and really was a gem. She not only cooked superbly, but looked after us all, decorated the camp tents with wild flowers, and was worth her weight in gold. Last, but by no means least, Jack, a pilot who had been flying for twenty years and at one time worked a trap line. His wife was also a fully qualified air taxi pilot – it seemed almost everyone we came across knew how to fly!

*The de Havilland Beaver, nicknamed the work horse of the north, is the favourite float plane.*

*John Hickey playing a large chum salmon – Twelve Minute Creek. Fresh from the sea these salmon fought magnificently.*

*A grizzly, one of six we saw in the morning – the guide thought it was around three years old.*

The week before we arrived at the Out-Camp Jack had been forced to shoot a grizzly, which had chased the camp dog and so frightened the poor animal it disappeared for two days. Returning, having failed to make a meal of the dog, the grizzly stood snarling and shaking his head and pawing the ground to get up courage, as Jack put it, to charge him. Armed with a small camera in one hand and rifle in the other he tried to frighten it off by firing over its head. When this failed to do the trick, it left him no alternative. I asked him if he had managed to get a good photograph but he said the light was very poor. Mine would have been very shaky. Grizzlies are, of course, protected except when it comes to just such a crunch and action is only taken with great reluctance.

Our stay at the Out-Camp was a brief two days. The first afternoon we fished a sea pool which chum and pink (humpback) salmon were entering in their thousands. But, like Atlantic salmon, they were only interested in the migratory urge to reach their spawning grounds, and we only caught a couple, before moving to the beach and fishing in the sea, which by then was a leaping mass of salmon all heading towards the river mouth. It seemed hardly a second passed before one or more broke the surface. It was amazing we did not snag one with every cast, so many were on the move – a sight we shall long remember.

That evening after supper we changed from ten-foot fly rods to light trout rods, and fished a long shallow pool on another river near the camp for sea run Dolly Varden, a type of char. We used a fly in the shape of an imitation salmon egg, lightly weighted to bump along the bottom in imitation of the real thing. Cast upstream the technique was similar to nymph fishing and if the line checked on the way downstream, striking soon let us know if we had hooked a fish or simply the bottom. These silvery fish, weighing up to 4 to 5 lb, followed behind spawning salmon, and being fresh from the sea fought like demons on the light tackle. All save one were released, the exception being a beauty we sampled for breakfast the next morning. It tasted to us rather like West Highland brown trout.

The next day John Hickey took us, with Jack as our pilot in the Cessna, to Twelve Minute Creek – so named for the length of flight time from the camp. We landed on a clear stretch of beach after flying through the surrounding hills and over a river which, at about 500 ft, showed a vast pod of salmon milling around in crystal clear water.

Fishing a tidal pool on the flood for an hour or two over another mass of chum and pink salmon was, as on the previous afternoon, not particularly productive, but one fish of about 8 lb took my fly – which went by the delightful name of Xmas Tree – made from flashaboo material. This fish provided our lunch, cooked expertly by John on an impromptu barbecue of gathered twigs and sticks, whilst we waited for the ebb. It had been an extraordinary experience to see literally hundreds of salmon splashing about and swimming almost through our legs whilst wading. But with the turn of the tide and the river flow exerting its influence to draw them upstream, the mood of the salmon changed dramatically and the fun began in earnest. They fought magnificently and gave incredible sport as they tore off line and cart-wheeled out of the water all over the pool. There were so many salmon it was impossible not to snag a lot of fish, all of which were returned. Sea lice clung to the underside of their bodies near their tails; John Hickey said he had never seen them fastened anywhere else, in contrast to our Atlantic salmon.

During the day four single caribou put in an appearance on the opposite bank, two of them stopping to look at us from time to time and on assuming no danger, trotted past in that effortless springy stride of theirs. One, the previous evening had actually walked towards us till quite close, as if enquiring what we were and why we were there. It may well have been its first sight of humans, for the nearest civilisation was 150 miles away.

That evening we again tried our luck on the sea-run Dolly Vardens in the clear still air, with the Pacific on one side and mountains of the Aleutian Range on the other, in utter peace and tranquillity. That we had been lucky was beyond doubt, for the temperature can plummet twenty degrees in less than an hour as storms sweep down from the north.

We flew back to the main camp the next morning above thick cloud for most of the way, but not before seeing a group of caribou below us. They were on a snow-covered slope at about 4,000 ft, chosen no doubt deliberately to get away from flies and mosquitoes.

These flights were one of the most fascinating features of our seven-day stay. In fact on our very first float plane flight to the main camp we witnessed the unique sight of two bull moose splashing out of a small lake, with two brown objects at the further end of the lake which I misguidedly took to be wild geese, quite forgetting we were flying at about 1000 ft. My comment on the moose to my companion seated next to me was overheard by Bill who was flying the plane, and he banked abruptly and flew back to have a closer look. My 'geese' were now swimming strongly in the middle of the lake, and proved to be none other than two grizzlies – the moose by then having sensibly disappeared into the surrounding forest.

*A bull caribou in velvet.*

*A 'pod' of chum salmon taken from our Cessna.*

On another occasion, whilst banking in our search for salmon below, we performed a neat little swerve to avoid two ospreys flying ahead of us – birds we saw every day. A pair of bald eagles also had a nest with three almost fully fledged young about 400 yards from the main camp.

The de Havilland Beaver – nicknamed the work horse of the north – is the favourite float plane. It can carry up to eight people, takes off at 55 mph and can turn virtually on its tail – very useful when spotting salmon which one usually does at a height of 100 ft or so. We must have travelled hundreds of miles during the course of our stay at the main camp, never once getting into a car for there were, thank goodness, no roads!

Coho, known as silver salmon, were by the end of July and first week of August, returning to the rivers of their birth and it was these fish in the main that had prompted our choice of time. Silvers are rated very highly as sporting fish, though it would be extremely hard to award them any higher honours in fighting prowess than the chum salmon we had caught earlier by the Pacific. Fresh from the sea they fought quite magnificently, and as one guide put it, are a very under-rated fish. It is a fact, however, that they are nowhere near as good to eat and have the lowest fat content of all Pacific species – hence their nickname dog salmon.

Wading was easy, so easy in fact that it was all too simple to forget what

*Bill Martin holding a beautifully shaped rainbow before release.*

we were about. After covering one particular stretch of water I climbed out to discover I had left my coat outside my waders and completely forgotten I had a Minox camera in the pocket. It was loaded with an almost completely exposed transparency film and 80 per cent proved spoilt – as luck would have it I had some duplicates on negative colour but the camera itself was wrecked – not very clever.

We were also particularly keen to fly-fish for the native rainbow and whilst fishing for silvers in the afternoon of our second day after a fly out from the main camp, saw across the river – at that point 80–100 yards wide – an almost continuous commotion of fish splashing on the surface.

Rainbows, we were immediately told, chasing and feeding on small fish.

The next day we float-planed in, transfered to an outboard jet boat, anchored in a very strong current, and proceeded to have one of the best morning's rainbow fishing of our lives.

Find silvers and reds (sockeye) and there close behind you will find rainbows waiting to gobble up the displaced eggs caused by so many salmon spawning together.

From mid-June when king salmon start to enter the rivers until mid-September, when the last salmon have died, the attention of all the non-anadromous fish is focused on the salmon, either consuming their eggs or pieces of decaying flesh after they have died. For die all of them do, unlike the Atlantic salmon. This period is known as 'the salmon shock'.

Our flies were not the egg imitations we had used for sea-run Dolly Vardens, but black with a flash of fluorescent blue, which was meant to resemble a leech. Cast across and slightly upstream and fished deep with a sink tip or fast sinking line, they proved immensely effective. The fly's name incidentally – a Woollybugger!

Native rainbows are a much prized asset and the whole area operates a catch and release programme to protect their stocks – a scheme many of us might well consider adopting for our own rivers.

Our largest rainbow would have weighed around 9 lb, but this was a small fish compared to the monsters caught both earlier in the season and later in September when, after a surfeit of feeding, a trophy fish could easily reach 15 lb.

It was interesting to record, whilst fly fishing for silvers, how gently they took the fly. In most cases it was barely perceptible, nothing more than an arrest in the line whilst drawing it in, and the deeper one fished the better.

*A native rainbow approximately 9lb – the largest we caught.*

We were joined by two American fellow fishermen that afternoon armed with spinning rods, and it was an eye-opener to see how lethal a spoon, toby or any type of bait was, for with almost every cast they seemed to hook a fish. Whereas we had to work hard for our silvers with a fly, and achieved reasonable success, theirs was phenomenal.

I could not help being reminded of the comment the then British Ambassador made when asked what he thought of the deal after America bought Alaska from the Russians in 1867 for 7,200,000 dollars. Well, he was reported to have said, Alaska is a very long way from England, it has a very long coast line to defend, and thirdly the salmon there don't take the fly! I wish he could have been with us. The deal incidentally worked out at just under two cents per acre!

# Chalk streams
# – the purist's water

ENGLAND IS BLESSED with many things – a fact we are inclined all too easily to overlook in the hurly burly of modern life. For the trout fisherman it is without doubt the famous chalk streams of Hampshire, Berkshire and Wiltshire with such names as the Test and Itchen, the Wiltshire Avon, Wiley and Kennet. Quite simply they are unique for chalk streams are found in few other places in the world and nowhere in America. There is a marvellous clarity in water filtered through chalk that has become, over thousands of years, the natural home of brown trout and no one will deny that fishing for them is a very special art, with all that a chalk stream provides by way of insect life. When I was first invited by a great friend to stay the weekend at his lovely mill house on the Wiltshire Avon it was a totally new experience for me after the spate rivers of the Western Highlands.

The mayflies were over on that first weekend, but I was greeted immediately by 'put your rod up quickly – we've got to catch four trout for our supper!'

It was one of those all too rare blissful evenings, without a breath of wind or cloud in the sky, when it felt just good to be alive. Up and down the river, little circles were appearing on the smooth surface, as trout and grayling were already rising to the returning fly. My host was without doubt one of the finest fisherman in the land, and I, by comparison, a novice. 'Put anything back under one pound' he said and whilst I watched him for a moment, he proceeded to catch a trout I'm sure would have scaled $1\frac{1}{2}$lb which I netted for him; to my amazement he put it back! Too easy I thought if it's like that, but as time progressed and the evening rise wore on, we had only managed to catch three more – and they were all smaller than the first one! As his guests had by then arrived, we had to be satisfied – in supermarket parlance – with three for four! He smoked them there and then and we ate them hot, the first time I had ever tasted trout cooked in this way, and they were quite superb.

Fishing there a few years ago when the mayfly were at their peak, we

*Fishing on the Longparish beat of the Test.*

were a bit late in getting to the river. When we arrived, another beautiful evening, we were greeted with the sight of the river covered with returning mayflies that just blanketed the surface. Not a trout rising – they had gorged themselves silly and we never even bothered to cast a fly, as it would have been quite pointless. Instead we counted mayflies as best we could – the number floating down stream from the bank for a distance of only three feet out – at the rate of 300 per minute! Cycles come and go, but this one was a really welcome return after years when, for various reasons, there had been a marked scarcity.

My eldest son, Anthony, who has done far more dry fly fishing than I have, has chipped in with the following.

Often after the first week or so of the mayfly hatch, the trout seem to get very choosy and difficult to catch even though they are rising strongly to the mayfly. I believe one solution to this problem may be careful observation of the rises even late in the afternoon and early evening when one might expect the trout to be on the spent gnat. Recently, on both the Avon and the Itchen, I have seen fish feeding on the mayfly nymph with the familiar 'bulging' underwater rise at 6.00 pm. and by switching to an emerger imitation have immediately induced a number of solid takes. When you see the trout splashing at the fly you can be sure that a normal dun imitation will be the best bet, and equally if you see quiet 'sipping' rises try the spent gnat, the deer stalker being a pretty effective choice. Do not think that spent gnat fishing is only effective in the evening – I have often had success in the morning, the trout feeding on the dead spinners of the previous day. Another common reason why anglers have difficulty rising fish is their nylon leader dimpling the water surface. This will put off educated fish that have seen many angler's mayfly imitations over the previous couple of weeks – I once had my eye wiped by a friend who had asked me on to his stretch of the Coln because of this. Thorough and frequent degreasing of the leader with Leadasink or Orvis Mud is the answer.

Catch and release is now practised on so many rivers, either voluntarily or compulsorily, and a lot of trout must fall for the artificial fly many times over. What I do find surprising is that a fish with a fly in its mouth will come again, often quite soon, after escaping.

I was fishing with another friend on the Longparish beat of the Test

OPPOSITE:
*Kingfisher Mill, a dream house on the Wiltshire Avon in late winter.*

when I saw several good fish in the Mill Pool at the edge of loose floating weed. The light wasn't too good and I thought when my fly landed that I had hooked a piece of weed, struck to clear it and left my fly behind. The following weekend my son Jeremy, fishing there with the same friend, caught a $2\frac{3}{4}$lb brown trout in the same spot and found my fly in its mouth. That pleased him a lot! I know this must often happen over the years, perhaps one of the most famous being the episode Edward R. Hewitt, the famous American trout and salmon fisherman, recounts in one of his books. He had been allotted a stretch of water by the Houghton Club at the mill above Stockbridge and on his way there his gillie told him about a very large trout living in the pool, which no one so far had been able to catch. It always fed in the centre lane among the weeds and was an extremely difficult cast. When they got there they saw a large trout rising regularly in its favourite place. As he put it 'it looked to me like a most difficult long cast to make but one that was possible with some luck'. It was evening and so he tied on a sedge and made several false casts below, then risked all to make the long cast into the centre lane among the weeds. 'The fly alighted just right above the place where the fish had been rising and floated down with some loose leader near the fly. As it passed over where the fish was, it disappeared,

OPPOSITE:
*The Wiltshire Avon at Lake in May.*

LEFT:
*This $4\frac{1}{2}$lb brown trout caught on a mayfly gave up and came straight into the net.*

RIGHT:
*A mayfly at rest during the day in early June.*

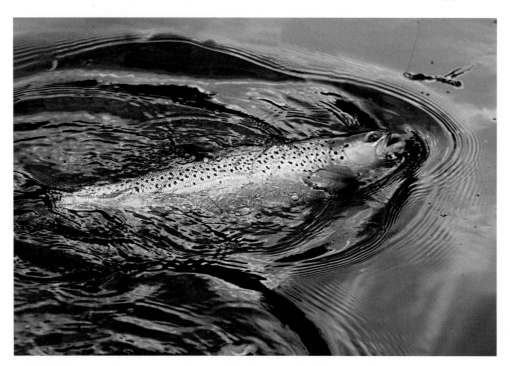

*Two from the Kennet, a 3lb rainbow and a 2³/₄lb brown.*

being sucked down quietly. I struck and was fast into the fish. Fortunately it did not go into the weeds but made for the open water below.'

He fought his fish from below and managed to tire it out and keep it clear of weeds and was finally able after a long tussle to bring it round to his gillie who was able to slip his long-handled net under it. 'I heaved a great sigh of relief when I saw it lifted from the water. When it was about four feet above it, it made a desperate struggle. It was too heavy and strong for the old net, which broke, letting the fish splash back into the water so that I still held it with the line passing through the hoop of the net. It was thoroughly frightened by this time, and made a straight dash for the weed bed where it parted the leader in one rush. I must say I did not want to lose this big fish, as I hoped to have one large one to my credit in the club book.' A year later when he again visited the Houghton Club he found the following entry in the club record book, dated a week later after the loss of his big fish. 'Trout, five and one-half pounds, from Mill Pool. Disdained by Hewitt!'

\*    \*    \*

OPPOSITE:
*The beauty of the Test, one of England's most famous chalk streams.*

With ever increasing demands for fishing, the stocking of many rivers has become a necessity, and there are few stretches left where genuine wild fish exist. There is no question that this has affected their fighting qualities when compared to true natives, and from what I have seen and experienced this particularly applies to hatchery-reared brown trout. A recent example of this occurred when my eldest son was fishing on the Wiltshire Avon. We spotted a large brown which he hooked with a mayfly first cast – although the mayfly season had finished and although it had not been rising at anything. It made one short feeble run, then to my surprise gave up and came straight into the net. It weighed over 4 lb. The water bailiff appeared almost immediately after it was netted and was scathing in his comments, saying quite rightly it was better out of the river – a view with which we both concurred. Apparently some large fish had been introduced by someone high upstream and had been finding their way down. A trout of ³/₄lb would have fought better.

*My son, Anthony, fishing the Itchen, near Kings Worthy, Winchester.*

By comparison rainbows fight like tigers and often seem to spend more

RIGHT:
*A grey wagtail, one of many lovely sights up and down so many chalk streams.*

BELOW:
*Lime hawk-moths mating in a bed of stinging nettles.*

time in the air than in the water. This was particularly brought out when, fishing the Kennet as guest of a lifelong friend one July morning a couple of years ago, I hooked a rainbow that jumped all over the river. A little later I caught a brown trout which made a couple of runs and then came straight into the net. The brown weighted 2³/₄lb exactly, the rainbow 3lb exactly. These were both hatchery reared but the difference was enormous.

*　*　*

Joining my eldest son who was fishing the Itchen near Winchester this year we had expected to see a good hatch of mayfly as it was the last weekend in May. I had to leave before the evening though a few mayfly were dancing above the tree tops by 4pm – but earlier, walking along the bank I found two lime hawk-moths mating – in a bed of stinging nettles of all places!

Whilst the mayfly is on, choice of flies presents little or no problem, but one evening some years ago whilst fishing the Wiltshire Avon in July, trout played extraordinarily hard to get and I don't know how many flies we tried to persuade them to 'take' that particular evening. All this is so delightfully summed up by Rodger McPhail in his brilliant cartoon which he has very kindly given me permission to reproduce.

by RODGER McPHAIL.

# The Bighorn River, Montana

BY ANTHONY LOWES

ANYONE WHO HAS TEENAGE CHILDREN will know the challenge of finding a summer holiday that all members of the family enjoy. It was by chance that I was talking with an American friend during a visit to New York City in early 1990 about this problem. He suggested we all might enjoy a stay at the HF Bar guest (or dude as the Americans call it) ranch, located near Sheridan, Wyoming, which he and his wife had visited for the previous 15 years. Now I used to ride 35 years ago, and as both our daughters are keen horsewomen, the idea of a visit to the second oldest dude ranch in the US situated, at 5,500 ft up in the Bighorn mountains in some of the most beautiful scenery in the West, started to sound appealing – particularly as I knew it wasn't too far from the Bighorn River.

*A view of the lower river.*

*Advice of regulations at one of the access sites.*

    I knew all about the Bighorn from an article I had read in the *Fly Fisherman Magazine*, when we lived in New York City during the early 1980s. That publication had billed it as possibly the greatest trout stream in the US, and I had resolved in my mind to fish it if I ever had the chance. Now was my chance – although I kept quiet about this with the family, as we were meant to be on a riding holiday!

    The Bighorn wasn't always this way. Until 1965 the river was one of the wildest and most dangerous in America. Having its source in the mountains of Western Wyoming, it flowed through a thousand foot deep canyon for 50 miles between the Bighorn and Pryor mountain ranges, and was capable of changing its volume dramatically often from hour to hour. Severe flooding was common in the broad valley beyond the canyon, and during the winter the river would freeze up, whilst in summer it was a warm water fishery, inhospitable to trout. All this was changed overnight with the construction of the Yellowtail hydro-dam near Fort Smith, Montana, which created a 70-mile reservoir, Bighorn Lake, to provide electricity, irrigation, sediment retention, flood control, etc. Water flowing from the base of the dam was now much cooler during the summer months and warmer during the winter, so that it remained ice free. And scouring from the spring run-off ice melt was no longer a problem, allowing heavy weed growth and abundant insect life to develop rapidly. This, combined with the limestone geology, created an ideal habitat for trout, and large trout at that. What began as a typical hydro/agricultural project created one of the finest 'tail-water' trout fisheries in the world.

Initially, the river was stocked with rainbows, but the few browns, already present before the dam, prospered unaided, such that today the trout population is approximately 5:1 in favour of browns, and has been totally self-reproductive for many years. So much so that in the first few miles below the dam, the population is approximately 6,000 trout per mile! And they're big, too, averaging around 2 lb or so, with the possibility of much larger fish from time to time.

With all this in mind, I had booked two weeks at the HF Bar ranch in early August 1990 and two days on the Bighorn with Paul Dubas, one of the then top guides from the Bighorn Angler outfitter and guide service. When you visit an unknown river I believe in hiring the best guides – it's money well spent in the end. After a tiring journey, with an overnight stay in Billings, Montana, we arrived at the HF Bar to a warm welcome from my New York City friend, 'Bronco' Jones and his delightful wife, Botsie, and

*The Bighorn Angler outfitter and guide service.*

were soon adopted by the group of their friends and ranch regulars, for the HF Bar has a 75 per cent return rate year after year. It's not difficult to see why. Set in the most magnificent scenery, and run impeccably by Margie Schroth, owner and hostess, the HF Bar combines wilderness with civilisation and, if you want to participate, the social life is good too. What's more it has two freestone streams that harbour a few surprisingly large trout up to 2 lb plus if you know where to look for them.

On the first day, the Bighorn Angler had asked me to be on parade to meet Paul Dubas at their shop in Fort Smith, near the dam, at 8 am. So, with 125 miles between the HF Bar and Fort Smith, it was an early start. Thankfully there is an excellent 'diner' in Fort Smith so I was suitably fortified when we met up. The Bighorn is a large, swift-flowing river, whose volume varies anywhere from 15,000 down to 1,500 cubic feet per second (c.f.s.). Generally it averages around 3,500 c.f.s, though this will entirely depend upon releases by the Bureau of Reclamation who regulate the flow from the Yellowtail dam according to environmental conditions. The river, for trout fishing purposes, is good for about twenty miles downstream of the dam with the top thirteen miles, or 'upper river', having catches restricted to 5 brown and 1 rainbow trout a day, with all rainbows over 18 inches to be returned. Most guides though practice 'catch and release'. This top section is fished heavily; but surprisingly the lower half, which often provides first class fishing just as good as in the upper river, is very lightly fished, but more about this later. Isn't it amazing how 'herd like' the human race is.

On this first day Paul chose to begin our float trip, for this is really the most effective way to fish the river, just below the dam. The boat used was dory style, about 12 ft long, most comfortable and effective for the job in hand. The drill is to float down on the current until you come to a pool, run or sometimes sidestream, where you get out and fish from the shore. Paul had already rigged up the two 9 ft-rods I had brought. One had a small weighted nymph/shrimp-like imitation known as a 'sow' bug and 'strike' indicator, positioned about 10 ft up the leader – this was a small fluorescent orange piece of balsa wood; the other had a pale morning dun dry fly, of which he told me there would be a good hatch later in the day. As we drifted down the river, I cast the nymph and 'strike' indicator set up about 20 ft out to one side of the boat, and was instructed to strike at the slightest movement of the indicator. Predictably, I missed the first take but was into a good two pounder soon afterwards that fought more like a three pounder.

*The sow bug and a 'crippled' pale morning dun.*

By the time we reached the first large pool, I think I had caught three browns on the nymph, around the 1½ to 2lb mark, and lost a larger fish that effortlessly broke me. Above this pool was a side carrier that looked very promising, and Paul changed the 'sow' bug for a minute midge pupa imitation, telling me to cast up into the head of the run. Second cast I hooked into a mini torpedo that rocketed down the pool, jumped to show its size, and broke the cast. It was a rainbow of 4 to 5lb.

We then went down to the main pool, where I put on a large muddler and caught a brown of about 3½lb. By this time the sun was well up, and it was starting to get hot, but that didn't seem to be affecting the trout. As we were beginning to see pale morning duns coming off, Paul was keen to go down to a favourite spot where he forecast there should be some excellent dry-fly fishing. Despite the heat in August, you can usually find some shade until the afternoon on the river, as its western bank is comprised of 30–50ft high cliffs, and there are many Cottonwood trees and Russian olive shrubs along the banks. There is much bird life in evidence too, particularly the red winged blackbird and least sandpiper – beautiful little birds; there are also ospreys around, though I never saw them. But watch out for rattlesnakes when you are picnicking – they are there, though thankfully I never met up with one.

Fishermen are not allowed to go more than a few yards away from the river because the land belongs to the Crow Indians, who closed down the fishery from 1975 until it was reopened by federal order in 1981. For a while, after the re-opening of the river in 1981, I was told, so hostile were the Crows to anglers that it looked for a while as if a second 'Battle of the Little Bighorn' might take place. In fact the real battle in 1876 took place between Sioux and Cheyenne Indians, rather than the local Crows. The battlefield is situated some 40 miles north-east of Fort Smith, and is well worth a visit if you have time.

If Paul hadn't stopped the boat, I wouldn't have realised the pool – if pool you could call it – was worth fishing. The bank indented slightly, creating a riffle that flowed over a shallow diagonal ridge about 30 yards long. The trout were lying behind the ridge in the deeper water and were rising sporadically to hatching pale morning duns. As Paul thought the hatch had only just begun, we decided to have a quick lunch. By this time the outside temperature was in the 90s, but the water was still only in the upper 50s, so wading was a welcome relief. In these conditions, it's essential to drink plenty of liquids, and top guides will always come well supplied. We drank gallons!

I was using a size 14 white hackled fly on a 5X tippet, which Paul explained was meant to represent a 'crippled' pale morning dun, a pale cream-coloured up-wing fly about half the size of our mayfly. Trout are meant to prefer the cripples as they are easier to catch, and so it proved. In two hours of non-stop activity, I must have caught a dozen browns around the 2lb mark and one beautiful rainbow of 2½lb or so. Talk about mind over matter, I had totally forgotten about the heat. However, once we left the spot, it caught up with us with a vengeance, and the fishing seemed to go off too. But I was hooked and couldn't wait for the second visit the next week.

After such a start, I expected the next time to be an anti-climax, but it wasn't. In the afternoon we hit a pod of large rising browns, which initially wouldn't look at the same fly that had been so successful the previous week. But when we changed down to 7X tippet, the action started – the fish had been put off by the glint of the sun on the 5X we were previously using. Several were over 3lb and we must have caught at least fifteen, all of which were released.

I have since fished the Bighorn on a number of occasions with other equally good guides, Bob Krumm and Dennis Fischer. I even persuaded our two daughters to join me, one of whom caught a 4lb rainbow during one of our days on the 'lower river' with Bob Krumm. But I think a day last year

*One we caught on the*
*Bighorn – 23 inches long.*

(1998) with Bob, who specialises on the lower river, was perhaps the most memorable. It was early August and the black caddis hatch was on in earnest. When I arrived Bob told me that he and his son Clint had discovered some new places on the lower river that might provide us with some good sport – an understatement as it proved. After catching a few 1 to $1\frac{1}{2}$ lb browns on 'yellow sally' stone fly imitations, Bob pulled in to a spot where the river was wide but no more than 3 to 4ft deep, so quite easily wadeable. I was instructed to move out about 25 yards into the main current and about a similar distance downstream, expecting to start fishing in the main current. But we turned back towards our bank, and Bob asked me to look carefully by a brier bush that came right down to the river bank. Sure enough we noticed a fish which Bob estimated at 18–20 inches long, very quietly sipping caddis no more than 6 inches from the bank. The trick would be to place the fly no more than 2 ft above it without catching on the brier or creating drag. To begin with I had a yellow sally/black caddis combination with the caddis tied on to the yellow sally about 18 inches behind, but one of the flies kept catching on the brier with its inevitable loss. After about 30 minutes of fascinating, yet frustrating, effort, we changed to a single caddis and I at last made the perfect cast. As the fish felt the hook it exploded downstream and put up a magnificent fight for the next five minutes. Not surprising, as it turned out to be a 19-inch rainbow in the peak of condition – about $2\frac{3}{4}$lb. Having safely returned it, we were able to retrieve some of the flies deposited in the brier!

After lunch we floated down to a side stream no more than 25 feet in width, and picked up three beautiful browns around the 17-inch mark. Moving on downstream we came upon a deep hole with a back eddy that could only be reached by disembarking downstream and making a somewhat hazardous traverse across a very steep bank. This meant that at one point we were 6ft or more above the river and from time to time were able to see through 'windows' in the water down into the eddy. What we saw made the pulse quicken appreciably – two 7 to 8lb rainbows in amongst a collection of browns up to 5lb! They were in the main stream just off the eddy, which was flowing strongly back upstream, so fly presentation would be a challenge. The best I managed was to drop my caddis towards the top and at the outer edge of the eddy, and after 15 minutes or so hooked a brown of about 2lb. By this time an afternoon thunderstorm was making its presence felt with frequent flashes of menacing fork lightning, so Bob felt we should take cover before it hit us. Later he told me he regretted not putting a big grasshopper on as this would have been more visible in the turbulence and might have brought one of the big fish up.

Once the storm had passed, activity quietened for a while, but around 7 pm we stopped below a tree that had partially fallen into the river. The branches that were touching the water provided the perfect spot for the female black caddis to lay their eggs, and the trout were aware of this too. Caddis were everywhere and so were the trout because the water was literally boiling below the tree – a sight I have only ever seen at feeding time at a fish farm when pellets are thrown into the ponds. There must have been so many caddis to choose from that for a while my fly was ignored. A savage take and surging run, before being broken signified that there were big fish amongst the pack. I eventually lost a 3lb rainbow at the net, after losing another large fish in a similar manner to the first one. Exhilarating stuff which was brought to an end when the light started fading and Bob had to row a further 5 miles downstream to our pick-up point. It had indeed been a memorable day.

The Bighorn season is effectively from March through to November, with the main dry fly fishing from July onwards. Whilst it can be very crowded on the upper river (though a good guide will always be able to find a spot to fish), it must rate as one of the finest wild trout streams in the world. If you find yourself in Montana, take a day with Bob Krumm on the lower river – a more pleasant and knowledgeable companion it would be hard to find.

*A fitting climax – returned to fight another day.*

# A week on the Miramichi, New Brunswick

THE WORLD FAMOUS MIRAMICHI, all four hundred and fifty miles of it, flows north-east through New Brunswick to discharge into the St Lawrence River and is one of the most popular and productive waters in Canada. The river system includes the main Southeast branch, little Southwest and Northwest branches and three main tributaries, the fast flowing Renous, the Dungarvon and the Cains. We were lucky enough to fish the Cains in late September; it provides a huge amount of water that in years past produced up to 25,000 salmon a season. Sadly this figure has fallen dramatically from its heyday and grilse – for which the Miramichi was always famous – dominate the scene.

It was to this setting six and a half years ago, and the Doctors Island Club at Blackville in particular, that my wife and I, along with Anthony, our eldest son and his wife, were invited by Don and Ann Calder. These American friends had first met Anthony while he was working in New York, many years earlier. A fishing rod is a splendid introduction and they were both fanatics!

The Club was beautifully situated on a small island, as its name indicates, fordable by car at one point in low water or by boat otherwise. Arriving in the afternoon, our first sight of the Home Pool was of a club member playing a grilse, which Kenny, one of several delightful guides, netted whilst we watched.

Because of the desperate decline in numbers in recent years, for a five-year period now ended, all salmon of over 26 inches had to be returned. This in effect meant that only grilse could be kept and the limit during our stay (1992) was two a day; when a further two were caught they had to be released, after which you had to stop fishing for the rest of the day. I believe very similar catch limits and restrictions still apply, and certainly all fish over 26 inches long must be released. The season has been shortened and now

*The beauty of the Cains River.*

*Kenny removing the fly
from the first ever grilse/
salmon caught by Verity,
our daughter-in-law.*

*The Home Pool, Doctors Island. The scene as we arrived – Lewis Harder, one of the members, triumphant, as his grilse is netted by Kenny.*

closes on October 15th – two weeks earlier than when we fished there. To help keep track of all this, plastic tags were, and still are purchased, and require to be fixed around the tail of any fish killed immediately after it is caught – heaven help you if you are found with a fish in your possession without a tag. Tough, but necessary conditions to build up adequate stocks for the future.

Wading was in most places easy and, of course, fly-fishing was the order of the day. The most effective fly went by the delightful name of Shady Lady – she had a black hackle and green butt. Others with equally emotive names were Butterfly and Copper King! I have no idea how many grilse must have run through our stretch during the week – I have never seen numbers like it – and when I asked Kenny how long the run had been going on he said non-stop since July! Just occasionally we saw a very large salmon leaping – certainly two I saw were of the 30 lb category – running fish I suspect, and nothing would tempt them. The Home Pool undoubtedly produced the most and the Blackville Town Fishing Club members had rights to fish opposite, which produced its amusing incidents. A long cast from a Doctors Island member could easily snag a long cast from the opposition. One always tried to avoid this by timing, but when it happened to me once, my fly was reeled in very quickly by my opposite number and released with puzzlement, for I was trying a shrimp fly and don't think he had ever seen one before. I was told afterwards they always wanted to reel in first just to see what fly you were using – but at that moment mine was not proving very effective!

The Club had fishing rights on a broad stretch of water a few miles below Blackville – Grey Rapids – which involved a short car trip and then boat to the opposite bank. It was a wide, fast flowing stretch of very powerful water and not all that easy wading. But it was the Cains River stretch, where the Club also had rights and where we went one day, that I really fell in love with. We never saw a sign of any salmon or grilse – it was then almost the end of September – due to the very low water levels throughout the late summer.

*Kenny, on our last morning, playing my small salmon in Goose Island Pool.*

Whilst fishing the Cains we were warned to be on our guard against patches of quicksand. I am glad to say none of us put our feet in it as I once did – and left a topboot behind – when very young in Perthshire. I hope most people know, if caught in quicksand they must throw themselves on their backs and 'float' – that way they cannot sink and can draw themselves out. But quicksands are frightening and a quicksand in one place can disappear and turn up in another, given the right (or wrong!) subsoil conditions.

The lack of fish was more than compensated for by the most spectacular fall colouring along the banks that was truly breathtaking. I suspect the next week would have been even more colourful – but is it not always thus! Suffice it to say the whole week was one of great enjoyment, made the more so by a camp run quite superbly by Brent Vickers, the camp manager who had taken over from his father Max; he was and still is a guide. Brent and I waded across for him to show me the Goose Island Pool a day or two before we left. It was secluded and free from opposition fly lines – a beautiful pool where I photographed Kenny, on our last morning, playing a grilse/salmon I had hooked there. This gives a little idea of what was in store next week. Autumn is one of my favourite seasons and when I said as much to Kenny he hesitated before agreeing. 'Yes' he said 'but it reminds us of what is to come'. – minus 20°C for months!

*The lack of fish was more than compensated for by the most spectacular fall colouring along the banks that was truly breathtaking.*

# Hill lochs - little gems of the Highlands

*'The true angler is almost always a lover of nature; if not he loses half the pleasure of his art. In following the river's course, he must of necessity pass through the finest and most varied scenery, and that too, at a time when beauty crowns the year. But enchanting as are the woodland banks of a quiet stream, there is to me a higher and yet more powerful charm in the solitary wildness or savage grandeur of the Highland loch. The very stillness of those bare hills and craggy summits, broken only by the rushing of some rapid burn that intersects them, has a tendency to elevate, while it calms the mind, and I envy not the man who could frequent such scenes and not feel them.'*

WONDERFUL WORDS by John Colquhoun taken from his classic *The Moor and the Loch*, written over 120 years ago. They are as true today as they were then, for who has not been moved by the beauty and splendour of a highland hill loch as it nestles like some hidden gem at the foot of a mighty hill, from which it often takes its name. Or maybe it is a little lochan lying unseen amongst the peat hags and heathery knolls of moorland in a dip of ground that renders it invisible until, having struggled uphill for miles, it appears like magic over the next brow. Your approach, if made quietly, will often pay other dividends – on one occasion we found an otter curled up asleep on a little island, and several times we have come upon red and black throated divers, and one year I surprised a greenshank which was nesting near the water's edge.

Two lochs at a height of just over 2,000 ft, both nestling at the foot of steep hills that rise to over 3,000 ft hold a mass of small trout, their size being determined by their number for there are far too many for the available feeding. During a hard winter these lochs are often frozen over until March. Insect life is thus inevitably restricted to late spring and summer. Viewed from above on a calm summer's day the surface often boils with a mass of small rings as little trout vie with each other for food. To cover the available water a boat is really a necessity and can provide non-stop sport,

OPPOSITE:
*A hill loch nestles like some hidden gem at the foot of a mighty hill.*

*A greenshank's nest in early May, a few yards from the waters edge.*

marvellous from the beginning. All the orthodox very small wet flies were generally seized hungrily but I think dark ones, like the Butcher, Zulu and Connemara Black were best. A 6-oz trout is a good fish and a half-pounder unusual – and just the job for breakfast!

Given the right conditions dry flies prove equally effective. In one particular lochan, at a lower altitude, greater feeding including fresh water shrimps, produce really worthwhile trout of up to four or more pounds. We have been forced to stock this recently as there was no spawning ground and thus no natural regeneration, and the stock was dying out. The addition of stock, fifty per cent of which were triploids which grow almost twice as fast as normal stock but cannot spawn – no matter anyway – is already, after two years producing trout that will weigh in excess of 3lb, and they really fight. The sight of a good brownie on a hot summer day leaping a foot out of the water at a passing damsel fly or daddy-long-legs is worth the trip itself!

OPPOSITE:
*A small hill loch – a little gem of bright water.*

Some years ago we stocked one particular loch with rainbows. I had been told many years before that this loch held char, but they turned out rather surprisingly to be perch. They must have waxed fat on the small rainbows, for several caught weighed $1\frac{3}{4}$lb – a size I suspect attained at our expense. However, two years after stocking with rainbow fingerlings, these had grown to $1\frac{1}{4}$lb, and six or seven years later one hooked recently on a dry fly jumped all over the loch and eventually escaped, but not before its weight was guessed at around 6lb. It is a fact that these rainbows have become, in the main, almost entirely bottom feeders. Whilst fishing there in August, the shallow end of the loch was literally moving with very small

*A beautifully marked $2\frac{3}{4}$lb brown trout.*

frogs, the size of a fingernail. We had to be careful where we put our feet for they were everywhere – there must have been thousands. In the tadpole phase many must have been gobbled up by both perch and rainbows, but still immense numbers survived.

It is a fact that the rainbows, when smaller, rose more readily to a fly. Now the fascinating point has emerged that we are again catching small rainbows, though we have done no fresh stocking for some years, and the only conclusion to draw from this is that they must now be breeding there.

Up until a year or two ago, stocking brown trout in one or two other small lochs has been on a very small and amateurish scale by the expedient of catching brownies from the burn and transporting them by bucket to their new home. This has worked remarkably well and they have not only survived but thrived in their new homes. This is in marked contrast to the sophisticated use of a helicopter to transport the stock. The delightful story goes that this method, used to carry some thousand or so – it may well have been more – brown trout to a particular loch was carried out in thick mist. After the event it was discovered they had been released into a loch of a neighbouring estate. When the owner heard what had happened he was not amused and demanded they be all removed from his loch immediately!

# Land of Fire and Ice – the Hofsa

WHEN I WAS ASKED if I could manage to get away to fish in Iceland at fairly short notice, I jumped at the opportunity to join the party. One of the conditions for all fishermen at that time, due to the outbreak of UDN salmon disease in our Scottish rivers, was that everything from waders and landing nets to fishing lines should be completely disinfected and a veterinary certificate obtained to certify compliance. This was a very sensible precaution; the Iceland authorities were taking no chances and with good cause.

Landing at Keflavik International airport it was a relatively short ride into Reykjavik. Despite all our clobber of fishing rods, nets and bags, Aylmer Tryon, who had got me involved, and I, elected to take the bus. We saw one that looked like ours and after much heaving and struggling managed to get two seats, sat down gratefully, only to discover we had boarded the wrong bus – the one we were on was booked for a special camping spree! We struggled out with our gear and eventually boarded the right bus – only to find I had left a thin line of rum down the centre of our previous bus, having cracked the bottle I had purchased at Heathrow especially for the trip! I hope they enjoyed the smell.

We stayed the night in Reykjavik and flew up to the Hofsa River the next morning, taking with us some huge plastic water-filled containers holding a quantity of parr sized salmon to augment those already there. Being a Sunday we were not fishing, for the owners, mostly farmers, reserved the day for themselves and made a family outing of it, with no holds barred when it came to fishing methods – mostly spinning.

Aylmer had arranged that he and I should have adjoining beats. He knew the river well, having been there several times and it was my first visit. We thus fished together, leap-frogging each other down the pools which enabled him to show me the water – quite invaluable for a new boy. Starting off on Monday I hooked a fish which I was sure was a grilse until I netted it and saw its mottled spotted sides and realised it was an arctic char of about 4¹⁄₂lb. We had it grilled for breakfast the next morning and it was superb – as good as any salmon or sea trout and a deeper richer colour.

Below our fishing lodge, an ugly but extremely functional pill box of a

OPPOSITE:
*Easy walking!*

139

LEFT:
*Hen ptarmigan; ever on the alert, this one had a family of chicks nearby.*

FAR LEFT:
*A northern golden plover – beautiful birds – they are remarkably tame.*

building with large picture windows on either side of the living room, was a little stream and pools that linked up to the river, home to phalaropes for the short summer months. It was for me one of the most fascinating parts of the week to see ptarmigan with chicks almost at sea level, golden plover, whimbrel and snow buntings all busy rearing their brood, and being dive-bombed by arctic terns the moment you got too close to their young. Virtually treeless except for the odd patches of scrub willow, the land at times presented a somewhat bleak appearance. It was saved by the river running through it with fast flowing gin-clear water and crumbling layer of rock – especially on the top beat on either side leading to the Foss itself.

It was fascinating watching from a high vantage point as Aylmer fished down one or two of the upper pools, while I sat with camera at the ready, to see a salmon 'take'. The whole action in such clear water was easy to follow, and the following season he took some wonderful cine footage of just that. Two amusing incidents fishing the top beat are worthy of recording. There was at that time no track suitable even for a Land Rover and our nearest spot to drive to was the end of the beat below. We then had to foot it up a rough track to the waterfall (Foss) – and foot it back with our catch. However, we were expecting assistance on our return journey from a young student/helper who was to meet us and ease our load of fish around the half-way mark. He did not appear until we had almost reached the Land

OPPOSITE:
*Taken on a cold drizzly day! The fight almost over.*

*Aylmer with the mink he killed with his wading stick.*

*Aylmer with his three salmon caught on the 'hitch' – 14, 13, and 13 lb!*

Rover and both Aylmer and I were by then tiring after carrying a considerable load of salmon and grilse on our backs. When he appeared he received a considerable broadside from Aylmer before being asked why he was so late! Spluttering profuse apologies he explained he had arrived much too early, and thinking he had masses of time had decided to try for a fish himself. He hooked a beauty and without a net followed it a long way downstream, fallen in the ice cold river, and looking like a half-drowned rat, had managed eventually to capture it. It weighed 19 lb – the largest salmon any of us caught that week! Poor chap, as soon as we heard his story it was all congratulations – he was indeed forgiven!

The other episode occurred on our way up, and was an unusual catch that Aylmer made. He was walking ahead of me when he suddenly broke into a trot, raised his wading stick high in the air and brought it down with a whack on a mink, killing it instantly. I never heard whether he claimed his bounty – $3 I think – the price these vicious predators then had on their heads from the Iceland authorities.

Whilst the weather had been overcast that day, with occasional drizzle which makes for a poor photographic record, the next two days were cold but sunny. Fishing the lower beats after a most enjoyable morning below our lodge Aylmer decided to try fishing the 'hitch' whilst I fished opposite him. It was just wadeable for me to cross. When it works, fishing the hitch is the most exciting way to hook a salmon as it comes at your fly like a porpoise. The great trick is to get your speed of retrieve right – not too slow so that the fly sinks and not so fast that it throws up too much water in front of it. I had just crossed to the other side and started fishing a bit above Aylmer when he hooked a splendid salmon and after a few minutes I asked him if he would like me to cross and net it for him. 'Yes please' came the reply so I waded over with difficulty and netted a salmon of around 14 lb. Having done so I waded back and started fishing again when exactly the same thing happened! I netted another beauty of about 13 lb and crossed over again, only to repeat the performance as he hooked yet another of about the same weight, which I also netted for him. By then it was time to call it a day – a superb bit of fishing and tremendous fun, and all caught on the hitch. Our last day together before I left – again on the lower water– was equally fascinating. Unusually for Iceland I imagine, the morning dawned without a breath of wind, the brightest of bright sunlight pouring down through the incredibly clear atmosphere and we spent the first two

hours photographing golden plover and whimbrel and generally relaxing in the Mediterranean conditions. Suddenly a slight wind sprang up and with it Aylmer who seized his rod and said, 'come on!' The ripples it caused were sufficient and he almost immediately hooked what must have been a large salmon. It played deep and led him quite a dance; eventually snagging on a rock it broke him. We neither of us even saw it.

Later that afternoon a huge grilse run came through – a splendid sight as one fish after another leapt out of the water on their way upstream. But they were so intent on running they wouldn't look at any fly we offered. On one of the last lower pools I fished, Aylmer filmed me fishing the hitch. The light was perfect and the salmon played up beautifully and his record of it marked a fitting end to my last full day. I had only time for a couple of hours fishing the next morning before Anthony, Aylmer's nephew, drove me over to the distant airport. Again bright sun and again fishing the hitch I must have gone near to catching the record for the smallest grilse anyone caught. It weighed just 2 lb!

OPPOSITE:
*The Foss. This effectively brings all salmon to a halt by its unjumpable height.*

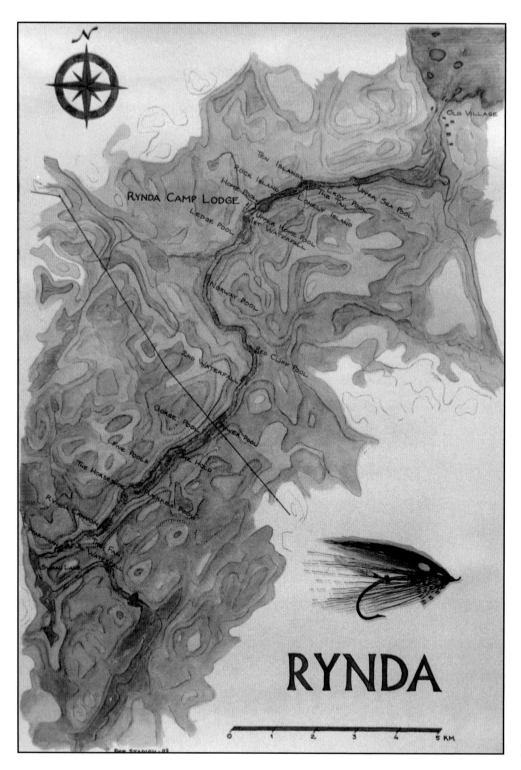

The Rynda, by Per Stadigh.

# Russian idyll

BY ANTHONY LOWES

WHILST I HAD HEARD A GREAT DEAL from angling friends about the fantastic Atlantic salmon fishing now available in Northern Russia on the Kola peninsula, catching large numbers of easy-to-catch fish has never been my scene. I very much enjoy salmon fly fishing, but I am probably more a trout fisherman at heart, generally preferring the challenge of matching the hatch and tempting large wild trout to take a dry fly. But few fishermen can resist the opportunity of catching large salmon if the chance presents itself, so I needed little persuading when my friend Don Calder suggested last September that I join him and his wife Ann, on a trip to the Rynda, one of the northern rivers on the Kola, in July this year. In prior years Don and the other members of the party had fished both the Rynda's sister rivers, the Kharlovka and Eastern Litza, and had caught and lost large fish up to 35 lb.

The Kola is a remote area to the east of northern Norway, situated largely above the Arctic Circle. Apart from the industrial city of Murmansk, it is a sparsely inhabited pristine wilderness. The climate is harsh with temperatures often dropping to below -30°C (-22°F) in the long dark winter; the Arctic summer, with twenty-four hour daylight, is short. In the south of the peninsula, the region is relatively flat and forested, giving way to the tundra and more hilly, almost treeless terrain in the north. The whole area is interlaced with unpolluted lakes, streams, and rivers, most of which are bulging with trout and salmon. In the south, rivers such as the Umba and Varzuga provide anglers with the chance to catch 50 plus salmon averaging 5 to 8 pounds to their own rod in a week's fishing. The northern coast rivers offer the chance of fewer but much larger fish, related to their cousins in the Alta and other big-fish Norwegian rivers.

In early July we travelled to Helsinki, overnighting there before taking an early morning flight to Murmansk, which was filled almost exclusively with over 150 fellow anglers. We arrived just before 11 in low cloud and mist. I had been warned to be patient as there were only two immigration channels at Murmansk airport, which first process the outgoing passengers (the previous week's returning fisherman) before admitting the incoming parties. Although I had been told that the reception would be unfriendly and facilities limited, things must be changing – not only were drinks available at the bar while we waited; we even received a smile or two from the immigration officials. By 2.30pm we had cleared immigration and customs, but now the weather was becoming a problem. After 2 to 3 weeks of heat wave, with temperatures up in the 30's, conditions had given way to rain, low cloud and poor visibility. The only means of transport to the Rynda camp, some 250 kilometres to the east, was by helicopter. These were not permitted to operate when the cloud ceiling was less than 350 ft and by 8.30pm, with no let up in the weather, it was suggested we spend the night at a hotel in Murmansk. Taxis appeared seemingly out of nowhere, and we were driven for 40 minutes at high speed in pouring rain to Murmansk – without a doubt the most hair raising part of our entire trip!

For my friends who had been fishing in Russia before, this was an unwelcome diversion at best, but for me, having never visited the country, the overnight stay in the Hotel Poliarnie Zori and the visit to Murmansk were fascinating. The drab uniformity of Soviet architecture and the rudimentary nature of the rooms in the hotel (one of the better ones in the city) was remarkable. Even so every room was equipped with a TV which picked up BBC World, Eurosport, and other foreign channels, all of which are now available to, and viewed by, the Russians themselves. Dinner was better than expected, but by 12.30am I was ready for a good night's sleep. The next morning all our minds were on fishing, and at noon, with the weather lifting, we were told to get to the airport as quickly as possible. The Russian MI-8 helicopter lifted off from the runway about 2.30pm, and in little more than an hour we arrived at Rynda camp, located some four kilometres from the mouth of the river. The camp is perched above a small lake through which the Rynda runs on its way to the sea.

We were greeted most cordially by our host for the week from the Northern Rivers Company. This Russian firm manages operations and owns the fishing rights to the three major salmon rivers in the area, the Rynda, the Kharlovka, and the Eastern Litza. There is also a fourth, smaller 'grilse' river, the Zolotya which is sandwiched between the Rynda and Kharlovka. All four flow north into the Barents Sea.

Once we had been shown to our individual wood cabins, we changed, and acclimatised ourselves generally, but our host was keen for us to get fishing. With the rain and cooler weather, conditions were improving after the heat of the previous week. Then the water temperature had reached 19°C, necessitating night fishing, though at this time of year it never gets dark, just slightly less bright than at midday. As we were to experience during the week, the weather can change from hour to hour, one minute bright sunshine with temperatures up into the 20's and the next driving rain with temperatures dropping into single digits.

The Rynda is about 100 kilometres long and accessible throughout most of its length to salmon. At the present time only the first 20 kilometres or so from the sea are seriously fished, though undoubtedly further pools will be discovered upstream as the fishery develops. The fishing is split into four beats, comprising about five main pools per beat. Beat 1 encompasses the Upper Sea Pool up to the Home Pool opposite the camp, above which Beat 2 starts and so on upstream. Generally transport is by helicopter and you are expected to be on time both for departure and pick-up. Forget all the talk you hear about poorly maintained Russian helicopters. We had a highly skilled pilot and mechanic who gave every confidence in their professionalism and attention to safety. The MI-2 helicopter, which remained on-site at

*The MI-2 helicopter at the Island Pool on the River Kharlovka.*

the camp, was perfectly suited to the role, with a capacity to carry up to nine people. But ear defenders were needed as helicopters are very noisy.

I was allocated Beat 3 by our trip leader, Lawrence Banks, and was paired with Mike Savage, a Kola veteran who has fished virtually every Kola river since it opened up, and who was a fund of information and knowledge during our time together. Although I had seen photographs of the Rynda in Roxton's brochure, I was not prepared for its rugged beauty. A fast flowing river, which over the centuries has cut its course into the boulder-strewn glacial landscape, it reminded me somewhat of the River Orchy in the West Highlands of Scotland, though it is less of a spate river: 11 per cent of its watershed is made up of lakes. The river has a huge variety of classic pools, rapids and falls up which salmon are able to ascend, leaving the fish less concentrated than on the Kharlovka and Eastern Litza, where impassable

*Mike Savage into an 8 to 10 lb salmon in the Falls Pool, Beat 4.*

*View from the main camp looking north to the estuary on the River Rynda.*

waterfalls prohibit upstream passage. Small birch trees are to be found along the more sheltered areas of the river bank, and dwarf birch grows over the rocky ground. A variety of alpine flowers, none of whose names I knew, were also much in evidence round the camp.

We arrived on our beat at around 6.30pm in driving rain and high wind, a blessing as I learned the next day, and were told that the helicopter would pick us up at 10.15pm sharp that night. Dinner would be at 11. Sergei, the manager of the camp, accompanied us and put us on to the top two pools (none of the beat's five pools have names). The house rule is that the first person to catch a 25 lb-plus fish in an unnamed pool has the right to name it. I was using a 15ft Sage rod, Valentine reel, and a new floating 10wt Rio Windcutter line, with a 9ft tapered 22lb breaking strain leader, attached to which was a size 1/0 barbless single-hook Bryson's Sheep fly which I had tied in London the previous week. The Bryson's Sheep is a black bodied fly with a long black and yellow hair wing overlaid with a rich yellow hackle, jungle cock cheeks, and a few strands of lureflash, which had proved effective on these rivers. This overall outfit was well suited to the river, and the Windcutter line proved to be aptly named in the strong winds that we experienced at times during the week. We had been warned not to use under

20lb leader as large fish often break these round the numerous rocks to be found in many of the pools. This is a sensible precaution as the fish at this time of year tend to weigh between 15 to 20lb, with a good chance of hooking, though not necessarily landing, a 25 to 30 lber. By mid-July the grilse start to come in, followed by a less prolific run of heavy salmon up to 40lb plus in September before the Arctic winter closes in.

I drew a blank in the top pool and walked down to the second pool already fished by Mike Savage, who had moved on down. Towards the tail in what looked lovely holding water my fly stopped, and moved steadily upstream. I was into my first Rynda salmon!

After I suppose a ten minute fight, I was able to beach and then release unharmed an estimated 15lb bar of silver. Before close of play that evening, I had had another 15 lber, again on the Bryson's Sheep, and Mike had caught a grilse and lost a large fish he estimated to be 18 lb, both of which came to a much smaller Ally Shrimp fly. As if to celebrate our success a rough-legged buzzard squawked overhead as we left.

In Russia all salmon fishing on the Kola is catch and release with only barbless single – or double – hooked fly permitted. Only the occasional grilse is kept for culinary purposes. In my view this is a thoroughly responsible approach to conserving stocks and the Russians are to be congratulated on these regulations. As an example of the wisdom of these controls, the experience on the Laerdal in Norway is instructive. The river had to be poisoned throughout its length to eliminate the *Gyrodactylus salaris* parasite that had infected the head waters, killing all juvenile salmon parr. The only cure is to eliminate all life from a river, then restock, and close it to fishermen for five years. Prior to the poisoning in mid-June, rods caught about 300 salmon that year. Only another 300 mature fish were retrieved from the river after poisoning, which surely proves how important it is to return fish unharmed when stocks are low, as indeed they are today across Britain.

The next day I was again teamed up with Mike and we were sent to the top beat, Beat 4. The weather was less windy and rather humid, an immediate invitation for the mosquitoes to appear *en masse*, and a head net became essential protection. Only Sergei seemed somehow able to tolerate them. We fished some lovely pools, but drew a blank until Mike hit a pod of 8–10 lbers in this beat's Falls Pool, and in quick succession had three out of exactly the same spot. I never even rose a fish all day, and was quite pleased when the helicopter arrived to whisk us away from the increasingly attentive

OPPOSITE
ABOVE RIGHT:
*The Upper Sea Pool.*

RIGHT:
*Home Pool.*

mosquitoes. That evening at dinner the rest of the party reported mixed success, which depended on which beat they had been fishing, a sure sign that fresh shoals of fish were beginning to run upstream.

The third day, Tuesday, saw me allocated to the lowest beat, Beat 1, under Sergei's exclusive tutelage. We first drew a blank on one of the most scenic of pools, the Rock Island Pool, which was within walking distance of the camp. When I asked Sergei if any of the pools had Russian names, he said many were unnamed but this one was called the 'Dancing Platform' in Russian, which given the topography of the pool seemed an altogether more apt and romantic description. Sergei was also keen to get down to the Upper Sea Pool about two hours before high tide as this was the best time to intercept fish coming in from the sea. However, before reaching there I picked up a 5 lb brown trout in a run, the only trout of the week. Whilst the Rynda does have some very good trout fishing with a plentiful population of fish up to this size in its head waters, fish to 12 lb or more are there to be caught on the Kharlovka and Eastern Litza above the falls impassable to salmon. Presumably the lack of competition for food from salmon parr accounts for the large size of trout in these rivers. We arrived at the sea pool in perfect time, and I decided to put on a large double-hooked orange Shrimp Fly, the thought being that a fish fresh from the sea might find a prawn or shrimp imitation attractive. I was right! Casting across intervening currents, a large fish immediately grabbed the fly, leaped right out of the water about twenty-five yards distance from us, and roared off across the pool. After a few minutes, when I thought matters were being brought under some sort of control, the fish decided to stop fooling around and headed at high speed back towards the sea, only for the line to go slack as the hook came out. A bitter blow as this was by far the largest salmon I had ever hooked, a fish we had both clearly seen and which Sergei estimated weighed around 27 lb. After lunch as the flood tide came in, I managed to lose one and raise two more fish, but it was a bit of an anti-climax after what had gone before!

Wednesday was a fishing day I will never forget. Paired with Elizabeth Banks, wife of Lawrence, we were dropped off near the top of Beat 2 in high wind and driving rain. Our guide was Misha, who spoke excellent English and, like Sergei, was a delightful companion. After catching a small grilse (which was kept for dinner) in, as Misha described, the Secret Pool since it was not named, we walked down towards that beat's Falls Pool. Suddenly, at no more than 50 yards, we came across a herd of about 75 reindeer, which had been sheltering from the wind and rain on a steep bank by the river. As they moved away we saw what looked like an albino amongst the herd, an unusual sight apparently. After this excitement, we soon arrived at the Falls Pool, a gorge which opened up into a magnificent very wide pool. As Elizabeth and Misha walked up to the head by the falls, I perched on a cliff 25 feet above the water half way down the pool and started to wet my Bryson's Sheep fly. On the second cast, a submarine emerged from the depths, totally missing the fly that was swimming just under the surface. Yelling to the others, I cast again and almost immediately hooked up into a heavy fish, which then proceeded to thrash around on the surface – an ominous sign that it was probably lightly hooked. We had just begun to manoeuvre down the rocks when once again out came the fly. Having had a good view of the initial take, I estimate I had lost another 25 lb-plus

*View along Beat 2 looking downstream.*

*Four flies, from left to right:*
*Bryson's Sheep, Tosh,*
*Orange Shrimp Variant and*
*Sunray Shadow.*

salmon. Two in two days was becoming a bad habit! We fished another two pools without further incident before the helicopter picked us up for lunch back at the camp. That afternoon our host wanted us both to concentrate on the Norway Pool, clearly one of his favourites. In two hours fishing we lost five fish ranging from 15 to 20lb each and all were on for considerable periods of time before coming off. Most came to a No.4 Bryson's Sheep fly, but any suitably sized fly would probably have worked given that these fish had clearly not been in freshwater for more than a very few days. I was beginning to think that barbless hooks were the problem, though Misha wanted me to strike and strike hard when the take was felt, a practice I had learnt in my teens that would generally pull the fly out of the salmon's mouth! In thinking about this, I recalled a conversation with another friend who had often fished in Russia and had had the same problem. He advised the use of single crab hooks with tube flies, as these hooks are off-set at an angle from the shank, and he had found they were more effective than standard hooks. I resolved to use a Collie Dog tube with one of these hooks the next day, particularly as a favourite fly on these rivers, called the Sunray Shadow, bears more than a passing resemblance to it.

When we returned to the camp that evening, we learned that we were not the only ones to have had some excitement that day. Lawrence Banks had been fishing the Falls Pool on Beat 4 when he hooked into a very large salmon on the far side of the pool that swam at high speed directly towards him, before turning tail and breaking his line on a rock as it tried to run out of the pool. On Beat 3 Lawrence's son, Richard, had hooked a fish that initially did very little, giving the impression that it wasn't big, before rocketing off downstream and ripping Richard's rod out of his hand into the river. His guide, Kolya, who saw the fish and reckoned it was another 25lber, immediately jumped in after the rod and managed to retrieve it safely, though by that time the fish had been lost. This action by Kolya was typical of the attitude of the guides and staff generally at the camp. They could not have been more helpful and we were looked after superbly throughout our stay. Even the cooking and food which I had expected to be mediocre was good.

As the Kharlovka camp wasn't full, Lawrence suggested that Ann and Don Calder and I should make a visit there the next day. The flight was a 15-minute helicopter ride and once we had picked up the head guide and manager, Volodya, we flew from the camp down to one of the best pools, the Island Pool, just above the sea. Because of the shorter length of river available to salmon due to impassable falls, fish were more concentrated in the pools than on the Rynda. The numbers caught during the week had been greater than with our party, but they too had experienced shoals of fish moving up river so that catches varied depending upon where you were.

The Kharlovka looked a less pretty and larger river than the Rynda, though I only saw a small part of it downstream from the camp. Nevertheless the Island Pool just reeked of salmon, though none of us could do other than raise one fish all morning. However, just before lunch, having put on a Collie Dog with the crab hook that I had resolved to do the day before, the fly stopped at the tail of the pool and a salmon of around 20 lb leapt out of the water. This time there was no mistake and after a 15 to 20 minute fight Volodya expertly beached an extremely fresh 22 lb salmon covered in sea lice. The fish was in superb shape, very thick and deep, and it zoomed off into the deep water once it was released after the mandatory photographs had been taken. My largest salmon ever!

*A 22lb salmon caught on a Collie Dog, with the head guide, Volodya at the Island Pool on the River Kharlovka.*

That evening after supper back at Rynda, we were offered the choice of flying down to the river's mouth to see an old mainly deserted village, or of fishing the Norway Pool for two hours. Don and Mike chose Norway and had a very similar experience to Elizabeth's and mine of the day before — four fish caught up to 20 lb. Meanwhile Elizabeth, Ann and I helicoptered down to the village where one of our guides, Kolya, still lived along with a couple of scientists who had a small cabin on the opposite side of the river. There were another dozen derelict but imposing wooden houses, originally inhabited by the local white Russians who were massacred, down to the last woman and child, during the Stalin era – a sobering thought that made us all appreciate how very lucky we were to have lived in stable democracies all our lives.

Our last fishing day, July 9, saw a large grilse run come into the river and in half an hour at the end of the day, two of our number hooked into five or six on the Home Pool where nothing had been happening earlier. Previously Misha had taken me up to Beat 4 again and we had shared in what I described to him over lunch as the perfect salmon fishing day – one fish in the morning and one in the afternoon. A salmon which turned out

*The Norway Pool, Beat 2 on the River Rynda.*

to be 13 lb rose from the depths of the beautiful Ptarmigan Pool to grab a long-tailed Garry I had put on at Misha's suggestion just before lunch; and one fish after lunch of 15 lb in the Falls Pool was taken on a large black and yellow fly called a Tosh. This was probably the same fish that had risen to a Bomber dryfly which I had dragged across the pool a few minutes earlier. During our lunch of excellent hot Russian soup and reindeer meat, we had watched a gyr falcon quartering the ground whilst we discussed many subjects of mutual interest.

When the helicopter picked us up, Misha was handed a note in English from Sergei which just said 'Go to Norway!' without any mention of the pool, which seemed to amuse him. This reminded me of the understated sense of humour of our Russian guides, best manifested the night before when a guide who had looked after one of our party the previous year dropped in from the Kharlovka camp. The two welcomed each other like long lost friends, and when inquiries were made of Sergei as to whether it would be all right to have a drink with this guide, the reply came back (given that there is a no alcohol rule in the camp for the guides) 'just one would be OK to support the conversation'. I couldn't have said it better myself.

Predictably at Norway we were into them again, landing a 15 lber soon after we arrived, and rising two more before leaving for the day. The pool was obviously packed with fish, as we frequently saw dorsal fins cutting through the water as the salmon moved upstream.

So ended the most wonderful week's salmon fishing, which had far surpassed my expectations. Our party had landed about 45 fish, but this gives a false impression of the real possibilities as more fish were lost than brought to the net, and the hot weather that had preceded our trip had undoubtedly reduced the number of fish in the river. The Rynda and Kharlovka camps, operated by the Northern Rivers Company, unlike I was told some other operations on the Kola, were superbly resourced and managed by the Russian team. This fishing must be the best Atlantic salmon fishing available in the world today, rivalling anything I had experienced in Alaska or elsewhere on my travels. I can't wait to return.